SUMMER MATH WORKBOOK

Bridge Building Activities

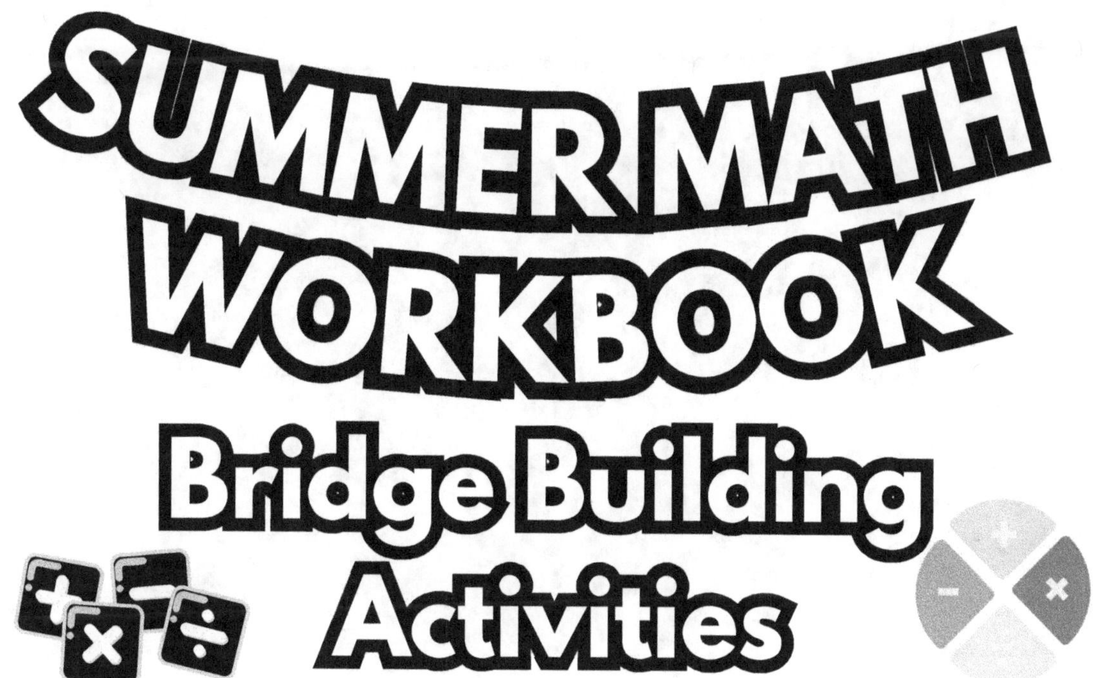

Introduction

As parents and educators, we understand the pivotal role that mathematics plays in shaping a child's academic journey and future success. Yet, the path to mathematical proficiency can often seem daunting, filled with challenges and complexities. That's where the transformative power of Summer Bridge Building Activities books comes into play, illuminating the way forward with clarity, precision, and purpose.

Summer vacation is a time for rest and relaxation, but it also presents the risk of the "summer slide," where students lose some of the academic gains they made during the school year. Summer Bridge Building Activities books are specifically designed to tackle this challenge, ensuring that your child stays academically engaged and prepared for the upcoming school year. These books provide a seamless bridge from one grade to the next, reinforcing essential skills and introducing new concepts that will give your child a head start.

Imagine your child eagerly diving into the pages of a Summer Bridge Building Activities book, greeted by clear, engaging content that demystifies complex mathematical concepts. With each turn of the pages, they embark on a journey of discovery, encountering thoughtfully curated practice questions that reinforce learning and sharpen problem-solving skills. As they unveil the answers to those questions, a sense of accomplishment blossoms within them — a tangible reward for their hard work and dedication.

Summer Bridge Building Activities books transcend traditional educational tools; they are meticulously crafted to build a deep and enduring understanding of mathematics. These books follow a sequential and logical progression, starting from fundamental principles and advancing to sophisticated problem-solving strategies. Each chapter is designed to build on the previous one, ensuring a solid and comprehensive foundation for future learning.

Parents, we yearn for nothing more than to see our children thrive academically and personally. We want to witness the spark of inspiration ignited within them as they overcome academic challenges with confidence and poise. Summer Bridge Building Activities books serve as indispensable partners in this noble endeavor, offering not just practice questions but the keys to unlocking a world of academic and personal opportunities.

Visualize the pride on your child's face as they master a challenging math concept, the joy they experience when their efforts yield results, and the confidence they gain with each success. These pages are designed to make learning math a positive, enriching, and deeply rewarding experience that will benefit them throughout their academic journey and beyond.

For educators, Summer Bridge Building Activities books are invaluable allies in the quest to cultivate mathematical proficiency in the classroom. Accompanied by comprehensive guides and readily available answers, instructors can focus on mentoring and nurturing their students, secure in the knowledge that these books provide a robust framework for effective learning.

Within the pages of Summer Bridge Building Activities books lies not just the promise of academic excellence, but the seeds of a brighter future. By integrating these resources into your child's summer routine, you are bestowing upon them the gifts of confidence, curiosity, and a lifelong love of learning.

Invest in your child's future today with Summer Bridge Building Activities books — because every great journey begins with a single step, and this step can change everything. Keep the momentum of learning alive over the summer, and watch your child soar to new academic heights.

Contents

Grade
1 2
SUMMER MATH
WORKBOOK
Bridge Building
Activities
Number Sense
Addition and Subtraction
Place Value

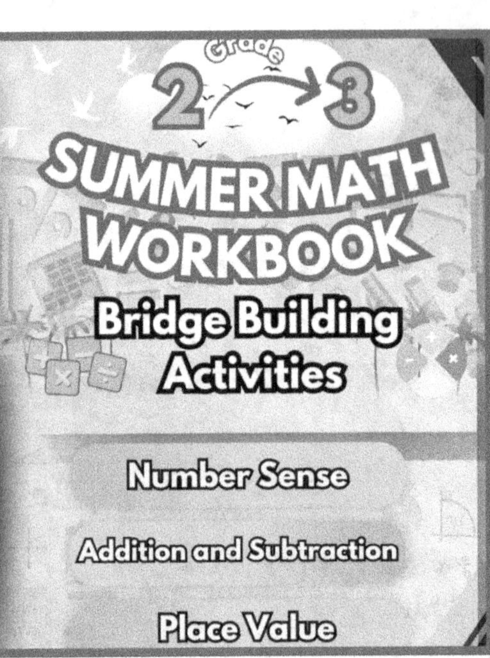
Grade
2 3
SUMMER MATH
WORKBOOK
Bridge Building
Activities
Number Sense
Addition and Subtraction
Place Value

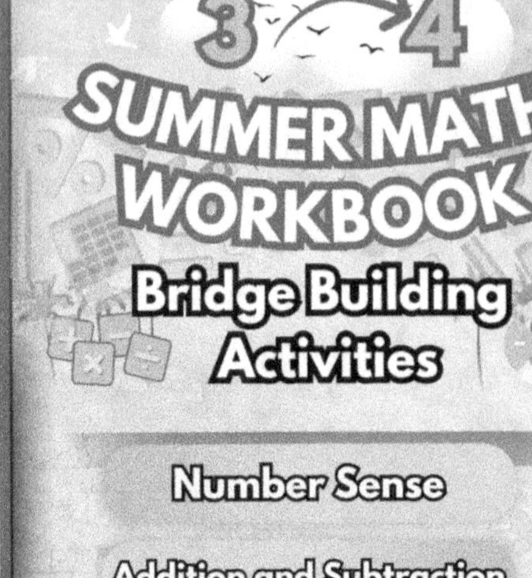
Grade
3 4
SUMMER MATH
WORKBOOK
Bridge Building
Activities
Number Sense
Addition and Subtraction
Place Value

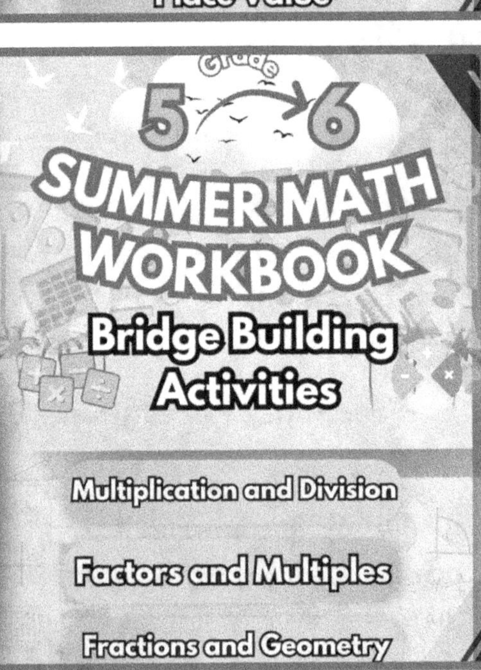
Grade
4 5
SUMMER MATH
WORKBOOK
Bridge Building
Activities
Multiplication and Division
Place Value and Units
Fractions and Geometry

Grade
5 6
SUMMER MATH
WORKBOOK
Bridge Building
Activities
Multiplication and Division
Factors and Multiples
Fractions and Geometry

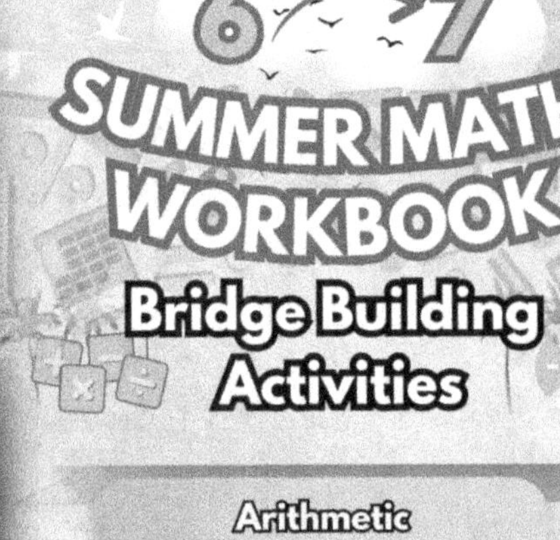
Grade
6 7
SUMMER MATH
WORKBOOK
Bridge Building
Activities
Arithmetic
Algebra
Geometry and Statistics

Grade
7 8
SUMMER MATH
WORKBOOK
Bridge Building
Activities
Ratio and Percentage
Algebra and Cartesian Plane
Geometry and Statistics

Grade
8 9
SUMMER MATH
WORKBOOK
Bridge Building
Activities
Ratio and Percentage
Algebra
Geometry and Graphing

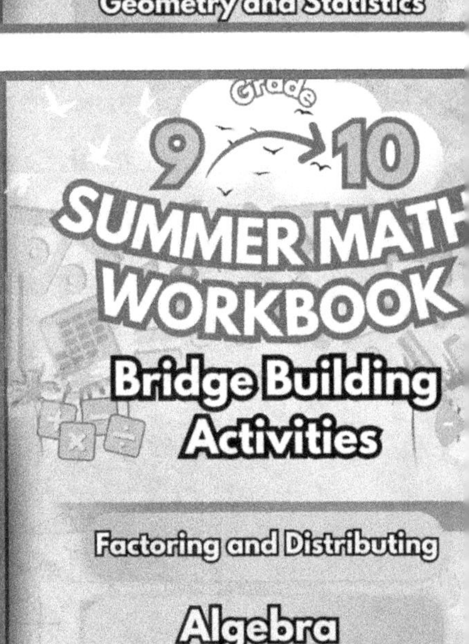
Grade
9 10
SUMMER MATH
WORKBOOK
Bridge Building
Activities
Factoring and Distributing
Algebra
Geometry and Graphing

Ratio and Proportion and Percentage

A proportional relationship between two quantities exists when they have a constant ratio or when one is a multiple of the other. In other words, if we increase one quantity, the other quantity will increase or decrease by the same factor. For example, if we double one quantity, the other quantity will also double.

Let's solve a problem:

$$\frac{\square}{9} = \frac{8}{18}$$

Step 1: Cross Multiply: Cross multiply by multiplying the numerator of one fraction by the denominator of the other, and vice versa:

$$x \times 18 = 9 \times 8$$

Step 2: Solve for the Unknown: Perform the multiplication on both sides of the equation:

$$18x = 72$$

Step 3: Divide Both Sides by the Coefficient of the Unknown: To isolate x, divide both sides of the equation by the coefficient of x, which is 18:

$$\frac{18x}{18} = \frac{72}{18}$$

$$x = 4$$

Step 4: Verify Check your solution by substituting x = 4 back into the original equation:

$$\frac{4}{9} = \frac{8}{18}$$

Since both sides are equal, the solution x = 4 is correct.

Percentage

Percentage is a way of expressing a number as a fraction of 100. It is commonly used to represent proportions, rates, and comparisons. The symbol "%" is used to denote percentages.

To calculate a percentage, we multiply the given number by the appropriate fraction or decimal equivalent.

How to calculate a percentage:

Convert Percentage to Decimal: If the percentage is given as a percentage value (e.g., 25%), convert it to its decimal equivalent by dividing by 100.

$$\text{For example, 25\% as a decimal is } \frac{25}{100} = 0.25$$

Multiply: Multiply the decimal equivalent of the percentage by the given number. This gives us the portion of the number that represents the percentage.

$$100 \times 0.25 = 25\%$$

Result: The result is the calculated percentage value.

For example, to calculate 25% of 80:

Convert 25% to a decimal: 25% = 0.25.

Multiply 0.25 by 80: $0.25 \times 80 = 20$. The result is 20.

Percent Word Problems

Percent word problems involve situations where percentages are used to calculate quantities or amounts. These problems often require converting percentages to decimals and then applying them to the given values.

For example:

Bella bought a pair of shoes for $90.00. If she paid an additional 90% for taxes, how much in total did she pay for the shoes?

- Bella bought a pair of shoes for $90.00.

- She paid an additional 90% for taxes.

Calculate 90% of $90:

Tax= 90% × 90

Tax= 0.90 × 90

Tax= $81

Add the tax amount to the original price:

Total cost= $90 + $81

Total cost= $171

<u>Pre-Algebra</u>

<u>Order of Operations (PEMDAS)</u>

The order of operations, often remembered by the acronym PEMDAS, stands for:

- **Parentheses**: Perform operations inside parentheses first.
- **Exponents**: Evaluate exponents (powers and roots) next.
- **Multiplication and Division**: Perform multiplication and division from left to right.
- **Addition and Subtraction:** Perform addition and subtraction from left to right.

The order of operations helps to clarify which operations should be performed first in a mathematical expression to ensure consistent and accurate results.

- **Parentheses**: Evaluate expressions within parentheses first. If there are nested parentheses, start with the innermost ones and work your way out.
    1. Example: $2 \times (3 + 4) = 2 \times 7 = 14$

- **Exponents**: Evaluate expressions with exponents (powers and roots) next.
    1. Example: $2^3 + 4 = 8 + 4 = 12$

- **Multiplication and Division**: Perform multiplication and division from left to right.
    1. Example: $2 \times 3 + 4 = 6 + 4 = 10$
    2. Example: $6 \div 2 \times 3 = 3 \times 3 = 9$

- **Addition and Subtraction**: Perform addition and subtraction from left to right.

    1. Example: $2 + 3 \times 4 = 2 + 12 = 14$

    2. Example: $10 - 4 \div 2 = 10 - 2 = 8$

Evaluate Expressions

Evaluating expressions involves substituting given values for variables in an expression and then performing the indicated operations to find the result.

For example: Let's evaluate $4x - 10$, when $x = 3$:

Step 1: Substitute the given value for the variable:

Replace every occurrence of x in the expression $4x - 10$ with the given value, which is 3:

$$= 4(3) - 10$$

Step 2: Perform the operations:

Perform the indicated operations according to the order of operations (PEMDAS - Parentheses, Exponents, Multiplication and Division, Addition and Subtraction):

$$= 4 \times 3 - 10$$

Step 3: Simplify:

Calculate the result:

$$12 - 10 = 2$$

Solving Equations (One Side)

Solving one-step equations involves performing a single operation to isolate the variable and find its value.

Let's solve an equation step by step: $16 + x = 31$

1. **Identify the Goal**:

    The goal is to isolate the variable x on one side of the equation.

2. **Simplify the Equation**: Combine like terms on both sides of the equation, if necessary.

    The equation is already simplified.

3. **Undo Addition or Subtraction**: If there's addition or subtraction involving the variable, undo it by performing the opposite operation on both sides of the equation.

    Since x is being added to 16, we'll undo this operation by subtracting 16 from both sides of the equation:
    $$16 + x - 16 = 31 - 16$$

4. **Isolate the Variable**: Ensure that the variable is alone on one side of the equation.
    $$X = 15$$

5. **Check Your Solution**: Substitute the value of x back into the original equation to verify that it satisfies the equation.
    $$16 + 15 = 31$$
    $$31 = 31$$

The equation is balanced, so the solution.

Equations (Two Sides)

A two-sided equation is an equation where both sides have expressions with variables and constants. The goal when solving a two-sided equation is to find the value of the variable that makes both sides equal.

For example: Let's solve an equation:

$$9 + 8x + 8 = 64 + x + 2$$

- **Combine Like Terms:** Simplify each side of the equation by combining like terms (terms with the same variable or constants).

$$9 + 8x + 8 = 64 + x + 2$$
$$17 + 8x = 66 + x$$

- **Isolate the Variable:** Use inverse operations to isolate the variable on one side of the equation.

subtract x from both sides:

$$17 + 8x - x = 66 + x - x$$

$$17 + 7x = 66$$

subtracting 17 from both sides:

$$17 - 17 + 7x = 66 - 17$$

$$7x = 49$$

divide both sides by 7:

$$\frac{7x}{7} = \frac{49}{7} = x = 7$$

- **Check Solution:** Once you find the solution, substitute it back into the original equation to ensure it makes the equation true.

Substitute $x = 7$ back into the original equation:

$$9 + 8(7) + 8 = 64 + 7 + 2$$

$$9 + 56 + 8 = 64 + 7 + 2$$

$$73 = 73$$

Find Numbers (Verbal Algebra)

Verbal algebra involves translating word problems or verbal statements into algebraic expressions or equations.

For example: The product of the two numbers is 91. One number is six less than the other. What are the numbers?

We're given a verbal description of a problem, and we need to represent it using algebraic symbols and equations.

Let's break down the given problem into algebraic expressions:

- Given that the product of the two numbers is 91, we can write the equation: $xy = 91$
- Also, given that one number is six less than the other, we can write another equation: $x = y - 6$

Now, we can use algebraic techniques to solve the system of equations to find the values of x and y, which represent the two numbers.

$$x(x - 6) = 91$$

1. **Solve the equation:**

   - Expand the equation:

$$x^2 - 6x = 91$$

   - Rearrange the equation into standard quadratic form:

$$x^2 - 6x - 91 = 0$$

   - Factor the quadratic equation:

$$(x - 13)(x + 7) = 0$$

2. **Find the solutions for x:**

   - From the factored form, we have two possible values for x:

$$x = 13 \text{ or } x = -7$$

3. **Check the validity of the solutions:**

   - Since one number is six less than the other, we discard the negative solution.

   - Therefore, the solution is $x = 13$.

4. **Find the other number:**

   - Substitute $x = 13$ into the expression for the other number:

   Other number $= x - 6 = 13 - 6 = 7$

So, the two numbers are 13 and 7.

Solving Inequalities

Inequalities are mathematical expressions that compare the relative sizes of two values. They are used to express relationships where one quantity is:

- "<" (less than),
- ">" (greater than),
- "<=" (less than or equal to),
- ">=" (greater than or equal to),
- and "≠" (not equal to) another quantity.

For example:

$$y + -10 \leq -8$$

To isolate y, we need to get rid of the constant term -10. Since -10 is being subtracted from y, we can undo this operation by adding 10 to both sides of the inequality:

$$y - 10 + 10 \leq -8 + 10$$

$$y \leq 2$$

To check the solution:

$$2 - 10 \leq -8$$

$$-8 = -8$$

The inequality is true when $y = 2$

Cartesian Plane

Cartesian Coordinates

The Cartesian Coordinate System, also known as the x-y plane, provides a method for representing points on a graph using two perpendicular lines: the x-axis and the y-axis. At their intersection, denoted by the letter "O", lies the origin.

To plot a point on this system, we use coordinates, consisting of two numbers. The first number represents the horizontal movement from the origin (x-coordinate), while the second number represents the vertical movement (y-coordinate). These coordinates are written as an ordered pair (x, y).

For instance, let's plot these coordinates:

$$A = (1, 3) \quad B = (5, 0) \quad C = (8, 6)$$

$$D = (9, 5) \quad E = (1, 9) \quad F = (3, 1)$$

$$G = (0, 8) \quad H = (4, 6) \quad I = (4, 9)$$

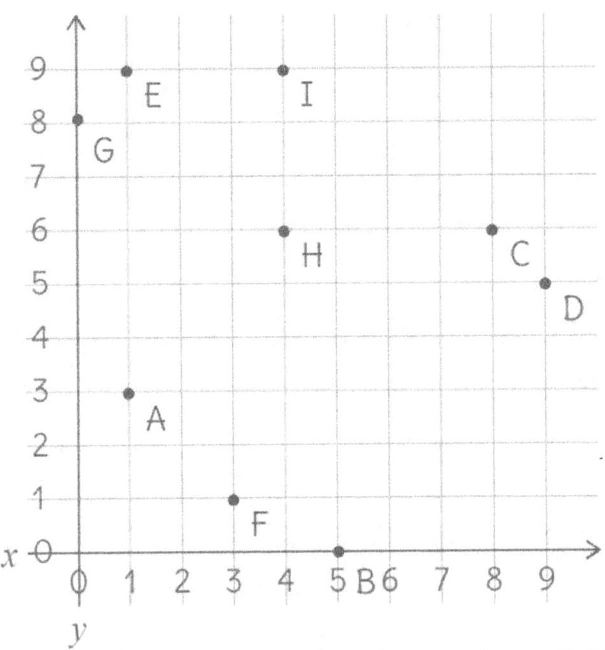

Cartesian Coordinates (Four Quadrants)

In a Cartesian coordinate system with four quadrants, there are two perpendicular number lines intersecting at the origin (0,0), dividing the plane into four quadrants.

To plot a point in this Cartesian coordinate system, we use an ordered pair (x, y), where x represents the distance from the y-axis, and y represents the distance from the x-axis.

For instance, let's plot these coordinates:

$$A = (-4, 1) \quad B = (2, 1) \quad C = (4, 2)$$

x
y
A
B
C
-5 -4 -3 -2 -1
1 2 3 4 5
5
4
3
2
1
-1
-2
-3
-4
-5

Geometry

Area and Perimeter

The area of a shape represents the amount of space it occupies. The perimeter of a shape is the total distance around its outer edge.

Area of Rectangle

For a square, since all four sides are equal, we only need to know the length of one side to find its area. We can calculate the area of a square by multiplying the length of one side by itself (squared). So, if the length of one side of the square is 's', then the area (A) is given by:

$A = s \times s$

4 in

4 in

$A = 4 \times 4$

$A = 16$

Perimeter of Rectangle

For a square, since all four sides are equal, we can find the perimeter by adding up the lengths of all four sides. If 's' represents the length of one side, then the perimeter (P) is given by:

$$P = 4 \times s$$

$$P = 4 \times 4$$

$$P = 16$$

Area of Triangle:

The area of a triangle represents the amount of space enclosed within its three sides. The formula for calculating the area of a triangle depends on the type of triangle. For a general triangle, we use the formula:

$$A = \frac{1}{2} \times \text{base} \times \text{height}$$

Where:

- *A* represents the area of the triangle.

- The base is the length of any one side of the triangle.

- The height is the perpendicular distance from the base to the opposite vertex.

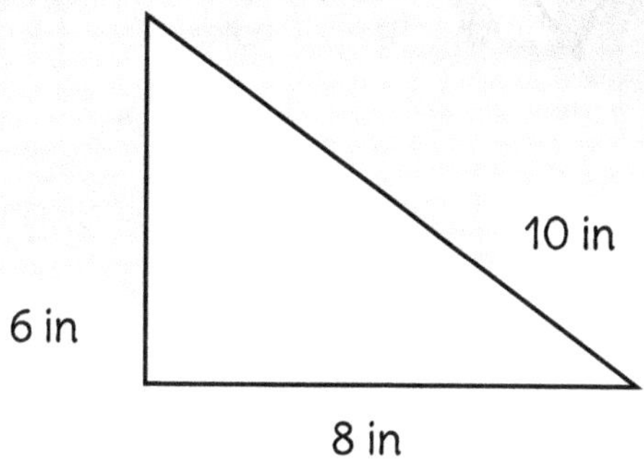

$$A = \frac{1}{2} \times \text{base} \times \text{height}$$

$$A = \frac{1}{2} \times 6 \times 8$$

$$A = \frac{1}{2} \times 48$$

$$A = 24$$

Perimeter of Triangle:

The perimeter of a triangle is the total length of its three sides. To find the perimeter, we simply add the lengths of all three sides together:

$$P = \text{side1} + \text{side2} + \text{side3}$$

$$P = 6 + 8 + 10$$

$$P = 24$$

Equilateral Triangle

An equilateral triangle is a triangle in which all three sides are equal in length. To find the area and perimeter of an equilateral triangle, we can use the following formulas:

- Area (A): $\frac{\sqrt{3}}{4} \times a^2$ where a is the length of one side of the equilateral triangle.
- Perimeter (P): $P = 3a$ where a is the length of one side of the equilateral triangle.

Area of Equilateral Triangle:

$$\text{Area (A): } \frac{\sqrt{3}}{4} \times (6)^2$$

$$\text{Area (A): } \frac{\sqrt{3}}{4} \times 36$$

$$\text{Area (A): } \frac{36\sqrt{3}}{4}$$

$$\text{Area (A): } \frac{36(1.73)}{4}$$

$$\text{Area (A): } \frac{62.35}{4}$$

$$\text{Area (A): } 15.59 \text{ in}^2$$

Perimeter of Equilateral Triangle:

$$P = 3a$$

$$P = 3(6) = 18$$

Isosceles Triangle

An isosceles triangle is a triangle with at least two sides of equal length. The angles opposite the equal sides are also equal.

Area of Isosceles Triangle

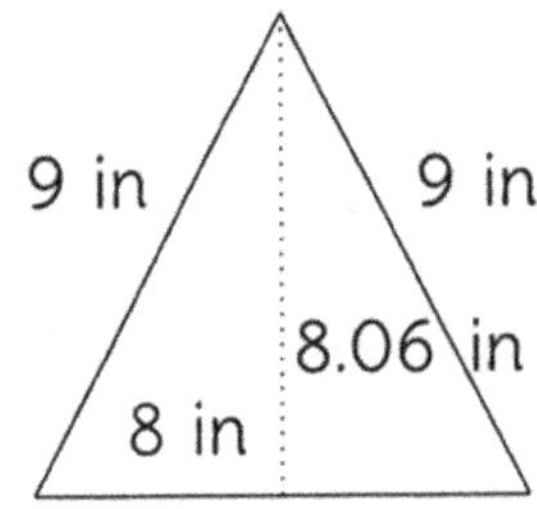

$$A = \frac{1}{2} \times \text{base} \times \text{height}$$

$$A = \frac{1}{2} \times 8 \times 8$$

$$A = \frac{1}{2} \times 64$$

$$A = 32$$

Perimeter of Isosceles Triangle

The perimeter of a triangle is the total length of its three sides. To find the perimeter, we simply add the lengths of all three sides together:

$$P = \text{side1} + \text{side2} + \text{side3}$$

$$P = 9 + 9 + 8$$

$$P = 26$$

Scalene Triangle

A scalene triangle is a triangle with no equal sides and no equal angles. The formula for finding various properties of a scalene triangle is as follows:

Area (A): The area of a scalene triangle can be calculated using Heron's fo rmula, which is given by:

$$A = \sqrt{s(s-a)(s-b)(s-c)}$$

where *s* is the semi-perimeter of the triangle,

and *a*, *b*, and *c* are the lengths of its three sides.

Perimeter (P): The perimeter of a scalene triangle is the sum of the lengths of its three sides.

$$P = side1 + side2 + side3$$

Let's find the Area and Perimeter of a Scalene Triangle:

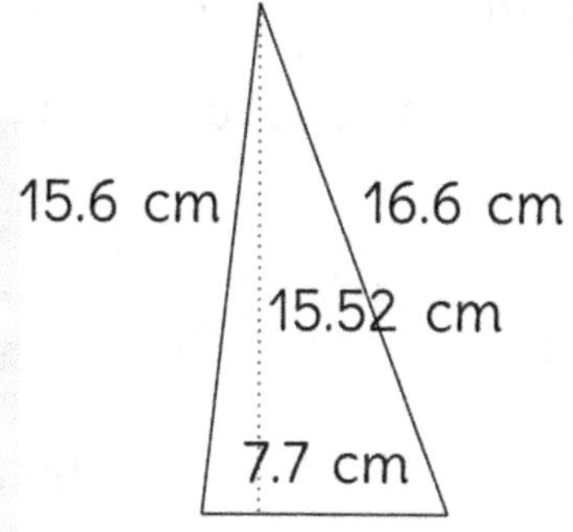

Area (A): First, we calculate the semi-perimeter (s):

$$S = \frac{a + b + c}{2} = \frac{15.6 + 16.6 + 7.7}{2} = \frac{39.8}{2} = 19.9 \text{ cm}$$

Heron's formula to find the area:

$$A = \sqrt{s(s-a)(s-b)(s-c)}$$

$$A = \sqrt{19.9(19.9 - 15.6)(19.9 - 16.6)(19.9 - 7.7)}$$

$$A = \sqrt{19.9 \times 4.3 \times 3.3 \times 12.2}$$

$$A = \sqrt{3445} \approx 59$$

Perimeter (P):

$$P = side1 + side2 + side3$$

$$P = 15.6 + 16.6 + 7.7$$

$$P = 39.8$$

Area and Perimeter of an L-shape

The L-shaped figure typically consists of two rectangles joined together to form an L-shape. To find the area and perimeter of an L-shaped figure, we will need to calculate the areas and perimeters of each rectangle and then combine them.

Area=Area of Rectangle 1 + Area of Rectangle 2

Perimeter=Perimeter of Rectangle 1 + Perimeter of Rectangle 2

Let's find the Area and Perimeter of an L-shape:

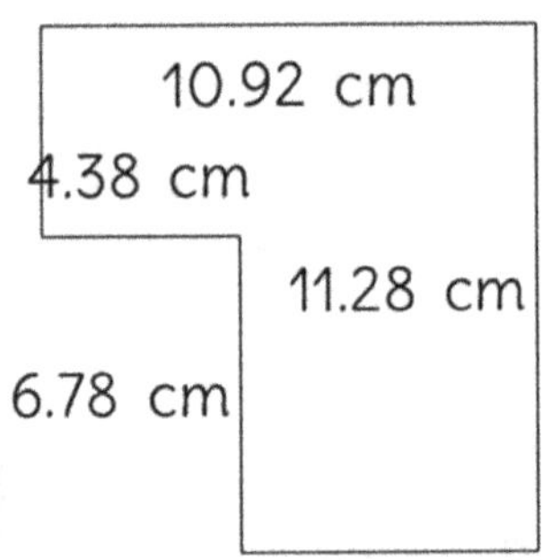

Area of L-Shape

$$\text{Area 1} = 4.38 \times 4.5 = 19.7 \text{ cm}^2$$

$$\text{Area 2} = 11.28 \times 6.54 = 73.7 \text{ cm}^2$$

$$\text{Area} = 19.7 + 73.7$$

$$\text{Area} = 93.481 \text{ cm}^2$$

Perimeter of L-Shape

$$P = 11.28 + 6.54 + 6.78 + 4.38 + 4.5 + 10.92$$

$$P = 44.4 \text{ cm}$$

Area and Perimeter of U-shape

U-shape is basically composed of three rectangles, we'll need to calculate the area and perimeter of each rectangle separately and then sum them up.

Area of the U-shape:

The total area (A) of the U-shape is the sum of the areas of the three rectangles:

$$A = A1 + A2 + A3$$

Perimeter of the U-shape: The total perimeter (P) of the U-shape is the sum of the perimeters of the three rectangles:

$$P = P1 + P2 + P3$$

Let's find the area and perimeter of the following U-shape:

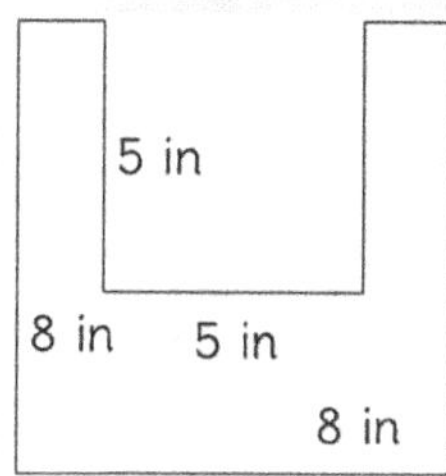

Area:

$$A1 = 8 \times 1.5 = 12 + A2 = 3 \times 5 = 15 + A3 = 8 \times 1.5 = 12$$

$$= 12 + 15 + 12$$

$$= 39 \text{ in}^2$$

Perimeter:

$$2 \times 8 + 2 \times 5 + 2 \times 8$$

$$= 16 + 10 + 16$$

$$= 42$$

Pythagorean Theorem

The Pythagorean Theorem is a fundamental principle in geometry that relates the lengths of the sides of a right triangle. It states that in any right triangle, the square of the length of the hypotenuse (the side opposite the right angle) is equal to the sum of the squares of the lengths of the other two sides.

$$a2 + b2 = c2$$

Let's use the Pythagorean Theorem to find the length of the hypotenuse (c) when $a=44$ and $b=78$.

$$c^2 = 44^2 + 78^2$$

$$c^2 = 1936 + 6084 \qquad c = \sqrt{8020}$$

$$c^2 = 8020 \qquad c \approx 89.554$$

Volume and surface Area

Volume refers to the amount of space occupied by a three-dimensional object. For shapes like cubes or rectangular prisms, we calculate volume by multiplying their length, width, and height.

To find the volume *V* of a rectangular prism, we use the formula:

$$Volume \ = \ length \ x \ width \ x \ height$$

Surface Area represents the total area covering all the faces of a three-dimensional object. For shapes like cubes or rectangular prisms, we find the surface area by summing the areas of all its faces.

The formula for surface area *SA* of a cube or rectangular prism is:

$$Surface \ Area \ = \ 2lw \ + \ 2lh \ + \ 2wh$$

Where: *l* is the length, *w* is the width, and *h* is the height of the object.

For example: Let's find the Volume and Surface Area of following rectangular prisms:

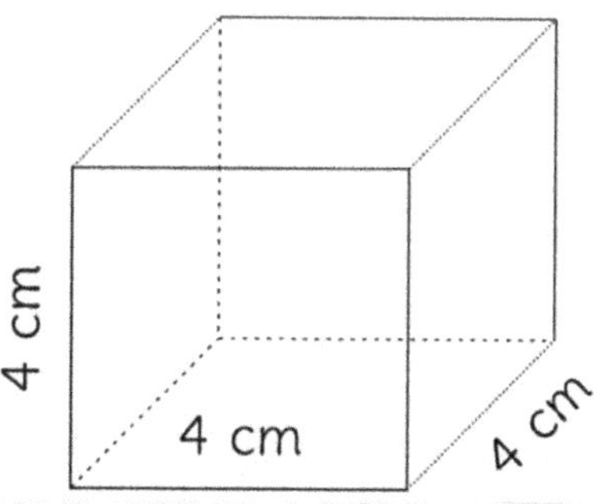

$$Volume \ = \ length \ \times \ width \ \times \ height$$

$$= 4 \times 4 \times 4$$

$$= 64 \text{ cm}^2$$

$$Surface \ Area \ = \ 2lw \ + \ 2lh \ + \ 2wh$$

$$= 2(4 \times 4) + 2(4 \times 4) + 2(4 \times 4)$$

$$= 32 + 32 + 32$$

$$= 96 \text{ cm2}$$

Different 3D objects have unique formulas for finding their volume and surface area. Here are some common ones:

1. Cube:

- Volume: $V = s^3$ (where s is the length of one side of the cube)
- Surface area: $SA = 6s^2$

2. Sphere:

- Volume: $V = \left(\frac{4}{3}\right)\pi r^3$ (where r is the radius of the sphere)
- Surface area: $SA = 4\pi r^2$

3. Cone:

- Volume: $V = \left(\frac{1}{3}\right)\pi r^2 h$ (where r is the radius of the base and h is the height of the cone)
- Surface area: $SA = \pi r^2 + \pi r \sqrt{(r^2 + h^2)}$

4. Cylinder:

- Volume: $V = \pi r^2 h$ (where r is the radius of the base and h is the height of the cylinder)
- Surface area: $SA = 2\pi r^2 + 2\pi r h$

5. Pyramid:

- Volume: $V = (\frac{1}{3})Bh$ (where B is the area of the base and h is the height of the pyramid)

- Surface area: $SA = B + \frac{1}{2}Pl$ (where P is the perimeter of the base and l is the slant height of the pyramid)

Statistics

Mean

The mean, also known as the average, is a measure of central tendency.
To find the mean of a set of numbers:

- Add up all the numbers in the set.
- Divide the sum by the total count of numbers in the set.

For example: consider the set of numbers: 70, 72, 49, 69, 27, 76.

$$\text{Mean} = \frac{70 + 72 + 49 + 69 + 27 + 76}{6} = \frac{363}{6} = 60.5$$

Median

The median is a measure of central tendency that represents the middle value
of a dataset when the values are arranged in ascending or descending order.
To find the median of a set of numbers:

- Arrange the numbers in ascending or descending order.
- If the total count of numbers is odd, the median is the middle value.
- If the total count of numbers is even, the median is the average of the
  two middle values.

For example: consider the set of numbers: 70, 72, 49, 69, 27, 76.

$$27, 49, 69, 70, 72, 76$$

$$\text{Median} = \frac{69 + 70}{2} = \frac{139}{2} = 69.5$$

Mode

The mode in statistics refers to the value that appears most frequently in a given set of data.

Let's consider the following set of numbers:

$$\{2, 4, 4, 5, 6, 6, 6, 7, 8, 8\}$$

In this set, the number 6 appears three times, more than any other number. Therefore, the mode of this dataset is 6.

It's possible for a dataset to have more than one mode if two or more numbers appear with the same highest frequency. In such cases, the dataset is considered multimodal. If no number repeats, the dataset is considered to have no mode.

For example:

$$\{2, 4, 4, 4, 5, 6, 6, 6, 7, 8, 8\}$$

In this date set, 4 and 6 appear three times. Therefore, this dataset is multimodal.

Range

In statistics, the range refers to the difference between the largest and smallest values in a dataset. It represents the spread or variability of the data.

For example, consider the dataset $\{ 68, 13, 30, 18, 45, 76, 11\}$:

To calculate the range:

1. Arrange the data points in ascending order.

$$11, 13, 18, 30, 45, 68, 76$$

2. Subtract the smallest value from the largest value.

- The smallest value is 11.
- The largest value is 76.

$$\text{Range} = \text{Largest value} - \text{smallest value} = 76 - 11 = 65.$$

Order of Operations (PEMDAS)

Evaluate Expressions.

1) $8 + 10 + 9 =$

2) $5 + 1 + 2 + 2 =$

3) $1 + 8 + 3 =$

4) $2 + 8 + 9 =$

5) $3 + 5 + 5 =$

6) $8 + 7 + 5 + 6 =$

7) $6 + 3 + 6 + 4 =$

8) $1 + 6 + 5 + 1 =$

9) $4 + 3 + 2 =$

10) $9 + 4 + 3 + 2 =$

11) $10 + 2 + 1 =$

12) $7 + 1 + 7 + 6 =$

13) $6 + 1 + 5 + 10 =$

14) $9 + 10 + 6 =$

15) $2 + 8 + 7 =$

16) $8 + 6 + 8 =$

17) $6 + 5 + 6 + 4 =$

18) $5 + 7 + 1 + 8 =$

19) $5 + 1 + 3 + 5 =$

20) $6 + 1 + 5 + 4 =$

21) $7 + 10 + 5 + 10 =$

22) $10 + 8 + 6 + 9 =$

23) $2 + 8 + 6 =$

24) $6 + 3 + 5 + 5 =$

25) $2 + 9 + 6 + 7 =$

26) $6 + 7 + 8 =$

27) $3 + 4 + 7 =$

28) $9 + 1 + 10 + 2 =$

29) $6 + 4 + 10 + 2 =$

30) $8 + 2 + 8 + 4 =$

31) $7 + 8 + 9 =$

32) $9 + 7 + 3 + 8 =$

33) $2 + 5 + 6 + 1 =$

34) $6 + 2 + 6 + 10 =$

35) $5 + 10 + 8 =$

36) $10 + 7 + 1 =$

37) $3 + 2 + 7 =$

38) $6 + 8 + 6 =$

Evaluate Expressions

Solve for the variable.

1) $-2 = y - 6$

2) $2 + z = 6$

3) $3 = x - 6$

4) $-1 = y - 5$

5) $-1 = z - 2$

6) $14 = 6 + z$

7) $4 - x = 1$

8) $-4 = z - 6$

9) $-4 = 3 - x$

10) $3 = 5 - x$

11) $8 + z = 9$

12) $8 - x = 2$

13) $-5 = y - 7$

14) $-3 = x - 9$

15) $y - 3 = -1$

16) $6 = x + 2$

17) $1 = z - 5$

18) $x + 3 = 12$

19) $4 = y - 3$

20) $1 = 9 - y$

21) $1 - y = -6$

22) $0 = z - 2$

23) $y - 7 = -1$

24) $z + 8 = 10$

25) $y + 8 = 15$

26) $8 = x + 3$

27) $x + 5 = 12$

28) $y - 4 = -3$

Solving Inequalities

1) $4 > y + -3$

2) $4 \geq 10x$

3) $-1 \geq \dfrac{k}{5}$

4) $k - -6 < 3$

5)
$$-6\,m \leq -8$$

6)
$$9 \geq -2 - y$$

7)
$$\frac{k}{1} > -8$$

8)
$$-9 < y + 7$$

9)

$$-4 \leq m - -6$$

10)

$$-1\,x < -6$$

11)

$$2 < 9 + x$$

12)

$$\frac{k}{-8} \geq -6$$

13)

$$-2 \geq \frac{m}{-8}$$

14)

$$-3 < -2 + k$$

15)

$$-1z > -4$$

16)

$$k - 2 \geq 3$$

17)

$$-1\,m < -2$$

18)

$$2 > x + 4$$

19)

$$7 \le \frac{x}{-6}$$

20)

$$y - -9 > -4$$

21)

$$-9 - m > 3$$

22)

$$8m \geq -6$$

23)

$$-1 \leq \frac{y}{3}$$

24)

$$5 > -8 + x$$

25)

$$6 \geq z + 6$$

26)

$$-8 \geq 2k$$

27)

$$\frac{k}{-3} < -9$$

28)

$$9 \leq 3 - m$$

Find Numbers

Think Algebraically and find the numbers.

1)   The difference of two numbers is 23. The larger number is 2 more than four times the smaller number. What are the numbers?

2)   The difference of a number and six is equal to 2. What is the number?

3)   The sum of two numbers is 30. The larger number is five times the smaller number. What are the numbers?

4)   One of two numbers is three more than the other. The sum of the numbers is 17. Find the numbers.

5) One-half of a number diminished by 3 is 5. Find the number.

6) The greater of two numbers is 9 less than two times the smaller number. Their sum is -6. Find the numbers.

7) A number increased by six is 9. Find the number.

8) One of two numbers is one-half of the other number. The sum of the numbers is 9. Find the numbers.

9) Nine less than a number is 1. Find the number.

10) Two-thirds of a number increased by 7 is 19. What is the number?

11) 24 is equal to the product of three and some number. Find the number.

12) Twice a number is 4. What is the number?

13) Find two consecutive even integers such that seven times the smaller decreased by the larger is 10.

14) Nine times a number is 0. What is the number?

15) Seven is equal to the quotient of a number and 4. Find the number.

16) One-third of a number increased by 3 is 5. What is the number?

17) Six more than a number is 11. What is the number?

18) The sum of a number and six is 7. Find the number.

19) One of two numbers is one-half of the other number. The sum of the numbers is 0. Find the numbers.

20) One number is ten times another. Their sum is 66. Find the numbers.

21) The product of two numbers is 96. One number is four less than the other. What are the numbers?

22) Twice a number is 6. What is the number?

23) One number is ten times another. Their sum is 33. Find the numbers.

Solving Equations: (One Side)

1) $0 = 4k - 12$

2) $4 + 10x = 84$

3) $z - 2 = 0$

4) $24 = 6 \times z$

5) $9 + 2z = 33$

6) $44 = 13z - 8$

7) $17x - 1 = 101$

8) $96 = z \times 6$

9) $9 = 41 - 2z$

10) $17 = 11 + 6y$

11) $13 = y - 6$

12) $k \times 20 = 20$

13) $m \div 20 = 16$

14) $z - 5 = 12$

15) $33 = 13 + 2y$

16) $7 = 133 \div x$

17) $21 = 3 \times k$

18) $y - 1 = 5$

19) $0 = x - 7$

20) $6 \times x = 120$

21) $7 = 330 - 17z$

22) $18 = 20 - y$

23) $4 = 80 - 19m$

24) $19 - y = 11$

25) $19 = x \div 13$

26) $14 - y = 13$

27) $27 \div y = 3$

28) $z + 7 = 21$

Solving Equations (Two Sides)

Solve for the variable.

1) $24 + k = 7k$

2) $5 + x = 2x$

3) $4 + 5x = 36 + x$

4) $7x + 5 = 2x + 20$

5) $2k = 9 - k$

6) $3 + 6x = 38 - x$

7) $3 + 8m = 7m + 9$

8) $7 + k = 2k$

9) $21 + 3x = 7x + 9$

10) $7 + 2m + 2 = 13 + m + -1$

11) $8 + 8k + 8 = 44 + k$

12) $8 + k = 2k$

13) $6k = 42 - k$

14) $5x + 4 = 1 + 8x$

15) $5 + m = 2m$

16) $3 + 2m + 6 = 19 - m + 14$

17) $16 - x = 1 + 2x$

18) $25 - x = 9 + 3x$

19) $13 + z = 6 + 5z + 3$

20) $81 - x = 8x$

21) $20 + x = 5x$

22) $4x = 3 + x$

23) $32 - 4z = 6 + 9z$

24) $8 + 3m + 3 = 17 + m + 0$

25) $5 + 2x + 9 = 17 + x + 3$

26) $5m = 12 - m$

27) $25 - 8m = 9m + 8$

28) $8x + 18 = 9 + 9x$

29) $28 + x = 5x$

Proportional Relationship

1) $\dfrac{6}{16} = \dfrac{42}{}$

2) $\dfrac{7}{20} = \dfrac{56}{}$

3) $\dfrac{2}{} = \dfrac{4}{10}$

4) $\dfrac{11}{13} = \dfrac{99}{}$

5) $\dfrac{1}{} = \dfrac{2}{22}$

6) $\dfrac{1}{6} = \dfrac{2}{}$

7) $\dfrac{3}{} = \dfrac{24}{112}$

8) $\dfrac{}{8} = \dfrac{16}{32}$

9) $\dfrac{8}{20} = \dfrac{}{120}$

10) $\dfrac{10}{15} = \dfrac{}{60}$

11) $\dfrac{1}{3} = \dfrac{3}{}$

12) $\dfrac{1}{2} = \dfrac{9}{}$

13) $\dfrac{4}{5} = \dfrac{8}{}$

14) $\dfrac{16}{18} = \dfrac{}{126}$

15) $\dfrac{2}{4} = \dfrac{6}{}$

16) $\dfrac{13}{16} = \dfrac{}{96}$

17) $\dfrac{7}{10} = \dfrac{}{90}$

18) $\dfrac{8}{} = \dfrac{64}{72}$

19) $\dfrac{8}{} = \dfrac{40}{95}$

20) $\dfrac{5}{12} = \dfrac{}{36}$

Percentage

Find the percentage of given numbers.

1) 300% of 100 = [ ]

2) 40% of 400 = [ ]

3) 90% of 500 = [ ]

4) 200% of 900 = [ ]

5) [ ] of 600 = 450

6) [ ] of 100 = 30

7) 1% of [ ] = 0.3

8) [ ] of 30 = 4.5

9) 100% of 300 = [ ]

10) 70% of 50 = [ ]

11) 80% of 200 = ☐

12) ☐ of 100 = 10

13) 6% of 200 = ☐

14) ☐ of 500 = 125

15) ☐ of 40 = 2

16) 2% of 400 = ☐

17) 50% of 200 = ☐

18) 9% of ☐ = 72

19) 35% of 800 = ☐

20) ☐ of 300 = 600

21) 80% of ☐ = 80

22) 1% of 800 = ☐

23) 6% of ☐ = 30

24) ☐ of 3 = 1.5

25) 40% of ☐ = 16

26) 60% of 100 = ☐

27) 9% of 600 = ☐

28) 5% of ☐ = 5

29) 3% of 300 = ☐

30) 10% of 900 = ☐

31) ☐ of 80 = 6.4

32) ☐ of 300 = 12

33) 7% of ☐ = 63

34) 2% of 700 = ☐

35) 20% of 700 = ☐

36) ☐ of 70 = 63

1) ☐ of 20 = 0.16

2) 0.5% of 61 = ☐

3) ☐ of 5 = 0.24

4) 0.4% of ☐ = 0.908

5) 19.7% of ☐ = 12.017

6) 15.9% of 599 = ☐

7) 0.4% of 494 = ☐

8) ☐ of 7 = 2.233

9) 0.9% of ☐ = 0.864

10) 6.3% of ☐ = 17.955

11) ☐ of 706 = 46.596

12) 9.6% of ☐ = 0.192

13) ☐ of 6 = 0.498

14) ☐ of 9 = 2.016

15) 0.1% of ☐ = 0.006

16) 3.7% of 75 = ☐

17) 25.3% of ☐ = 59.455

18) 0.4% of ☐ = 3.976

19) [   ] of 2 = 0.014

20) 9.2% of 47 = [   ]

21) 0.1% of 3 = [   ]

22) [   ] of 27 = 4.239

23) [   ] of 8 = 0.72

24) 0.6% of 596 = [   ]

25) 8.9% of 317 = [   ]

26) [   ] of 2 = 0.008

27) 0.6% of 60 = [   ]

28) [   ] of 8 = 0.04

29) 0.9% of 302 = ☐

30) 47.2% of ☐ = 25.016

31) 0.7% of ☐ = 0.686

32) 0.6% of 7 = ☐

33) 4.2% of 2 = ☐

34) ☐ of 690 = 5.52

35) 0.5% of 114 = ☐

36) ☐ of 58 = 2.784

37) 0.4% of 55 = ☐

38) 19.7% of ☐ = 0.985

Ratio Conversions

1)

	Ratio	Fraction	Percent	Decimal
a.			23.5%	
b.	4:14			
c.	1:1			
d.			20%	
e.	3:9			
f.		6/15		
g.			5.6%	
h.	5:17			
i.		12/20		
j.				0.167
k.				0.05
l.			7.7%	
m.			40%	
n.	1:3			
o.			13.3%	

2)

	Ratio	Fraction	Percent	Decimal
a.	5:7			
b.		2/2		
c.			81.8%	
d.	6:20			
e.			80%	
f.			85.7%	
g.		4/12		
h.			61.5%	
i.			20%	
j.	18:20			
k.			28.6%	
l.	9:13			
m.	1:2			
n.		16/19		
o.		2/17		

3)

	Ratio	Fraction	Percent	Decimal
a.		1/4		
b.	8:11			
c.				0.75
d.		1/16		
e.		7/15		
f.			85.7%	
g.				0.182
h.				0.235
i.		3/14		
j.	6:14			
k.	9:10			
l.			76.9%	
m.			64.3%	
n.	15:19			
o.	6:10			

Cartesian Coordinates

Fill in as indicated.

1)

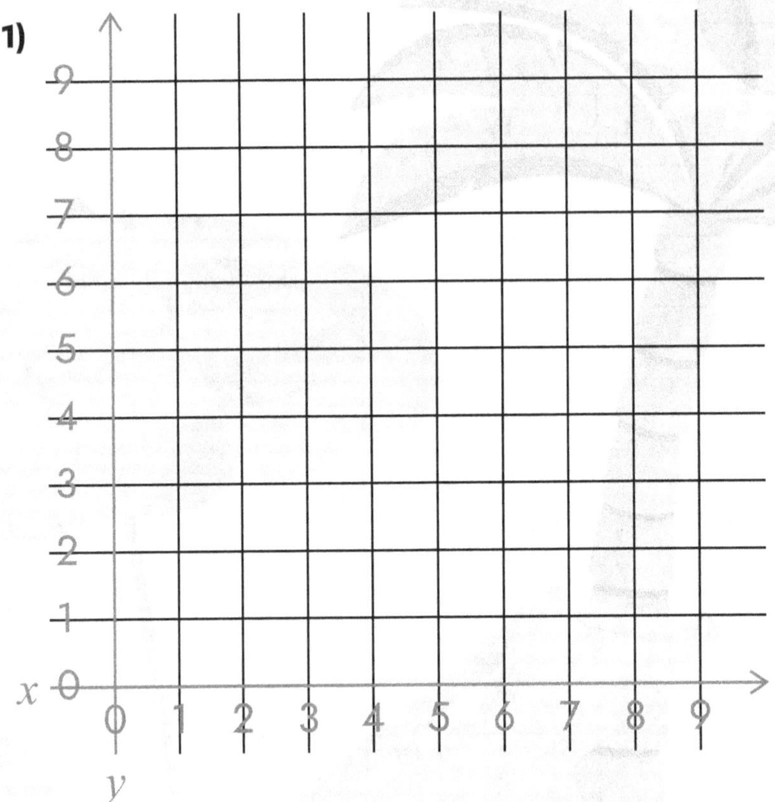

A = (4, 1)   B = (5, 3)   C = (6, 5)

D = (3, 2)   E = (7, 4)   F = (8, 8)

G = (5, 7)   H = (1, 4)   I = (6, 3)

2)

A = (9, 5)   B = (0, 4)   C = (0, 1)

D = (4, 6)   E = (5, 8)   F = (3, 9)

G = (6, 6)   H = (6, 3)   I = (5, 1)

3)

A = (0, 1)   B = (3, 8)   C = (7, 4)

D = (9, 1)   E = (7, 6)   F = (5, 2)

G = (6, 0)   H = (9, 0)   I = (2, 0)

4)

A = (2, 2) B = (4, 1) C = (8, 9)

D = (8, 4) E = (8, 7) F = (7, 1)

G = (2, 1) H = (1, 0) I = (4, 4)

5)

A = (9, 0)   B = (7, 6)   C = (5, 9)

D = (4, 7)   E = (0, 3)   F = (2, 3)

G = (0, 5)   H = (4, 5)   I = (1, 3)

Cartesian Coordinates

Fill in as indicated.

1)
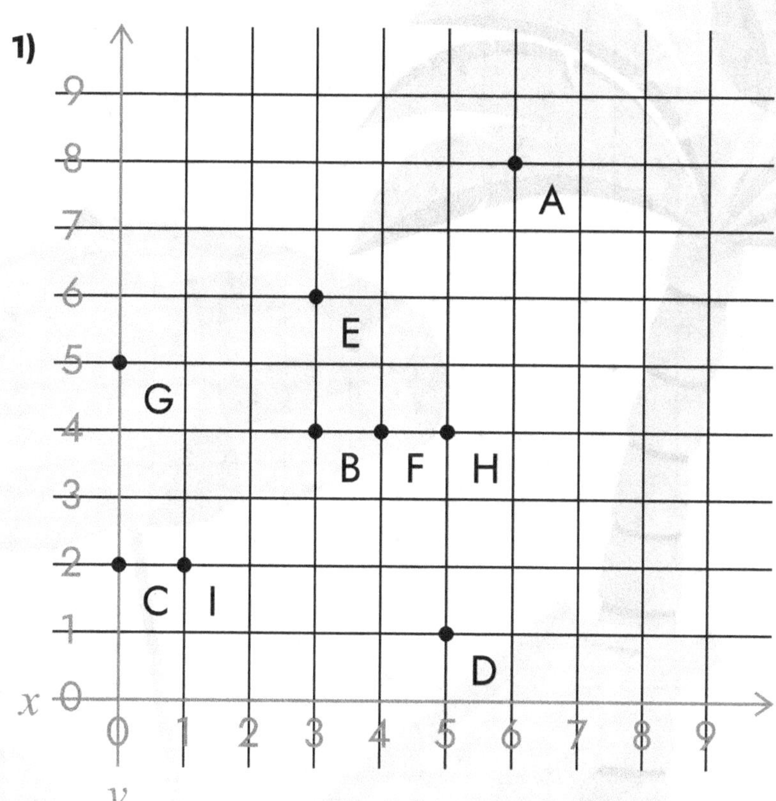

A = ________   B = ________   C = ________

D = ________   E = ________   F = ________

G = ________   H = ________   I = ________

2)

A = _______ B = _______ C = _______

D = _______ E = _______ F = _______

G = _______ H = _______ I = _______

SUMMER MATH WORKBOOK
NAME:
BUILDING ACTIVITIES

3)

9
C
8
7
G
6
E
5
F   B
4
3
A   H
2
1
D
x 0
0 1 2 3 4 5 6 7 8 9
y

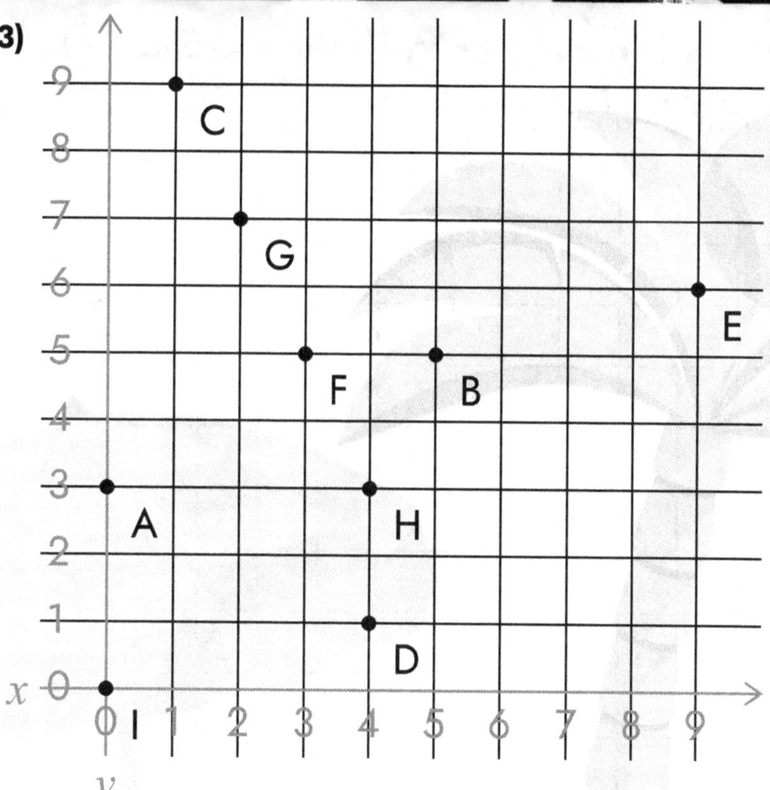

A = _______   B = _______   C = _______

D = _______   E = _______   F = _______

G = _______   H = _______   I = _______

Cartesian Coordinates With Four Quadrants

Fill in as indicated.

1)

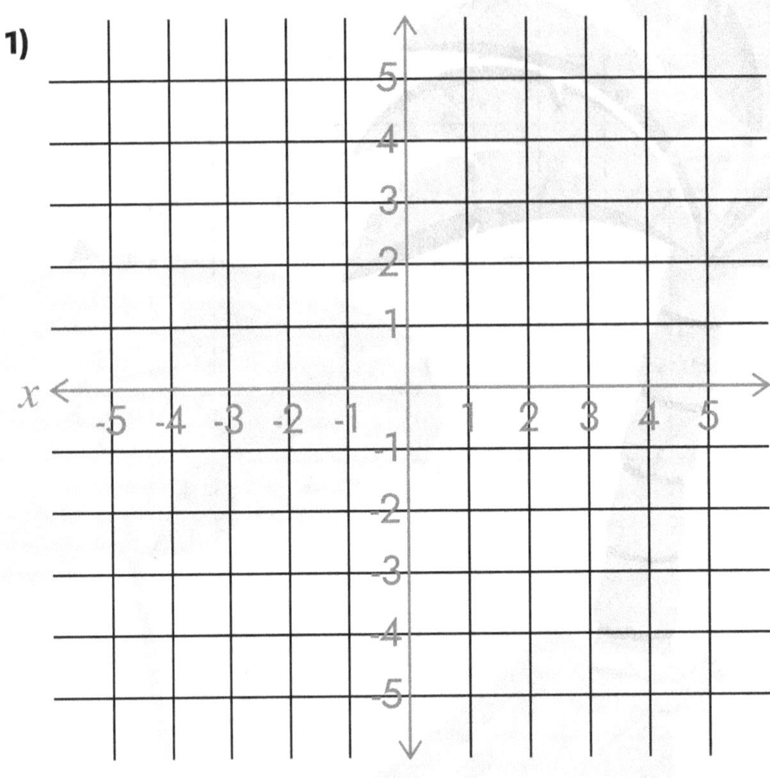

A = (1, -3)   B = (-3, 0)   C = (3, -4)

D = (2, 0)   E = (-1, 0)   F = (-3, -2)

G = (1, 3)   H = (5, -1)   I = (-1, -4)

2)

A = (5, -1)   B = (3, 2)   C = (-3, -4)

D = (0, 4)   E = (-3, 4)   F = (5, 1)

G = (-5, -2)   H = (-5, -5)   I = (2, -2)

3)

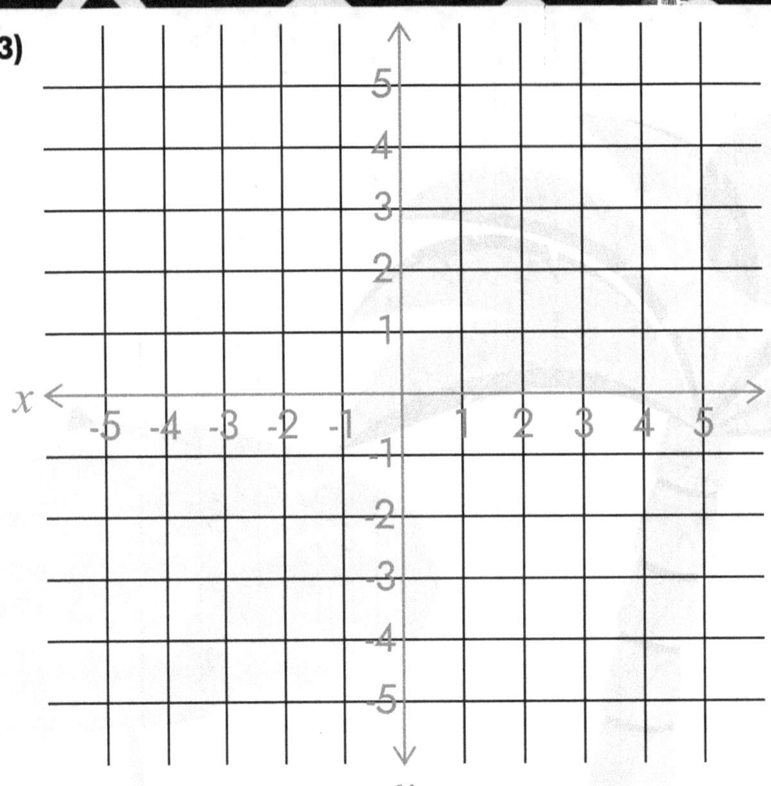

A = (-1, 1)   B = (-3, -3)   C = (-1, 0)

D = (-2, 5)   E = (4, 4)   F = (1, 3)

G = (-2, -2)   H = (-1, 2)   I = (-5, -5)

Cartesian Coordinates With Four Quadrants

Fill in as indicated.

1)

A = _______   B = _______   C = _______

D = _______   E = _______   F = _______

G = _______   H = _______   I = _______

2)

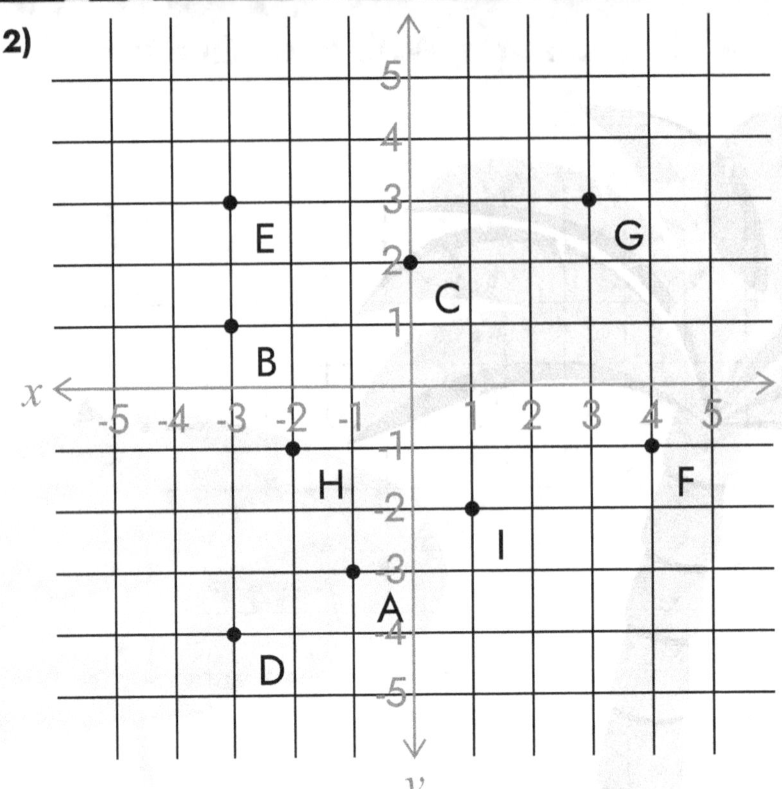

A = _______   B = _______   C = _______

D = _______   E = _______   F = _______

G = _______   H = _______   I = _______

SUMMER MATH WORKBOOK
NAME:
BUILDING ACTIVITIES

3)

5
4 C
3 D
2 G I
1
A
x
-5 -4 -3 -2 -1   1 2 3 F 4 5 B
-1
-2
-3
-4
-5 E H
y

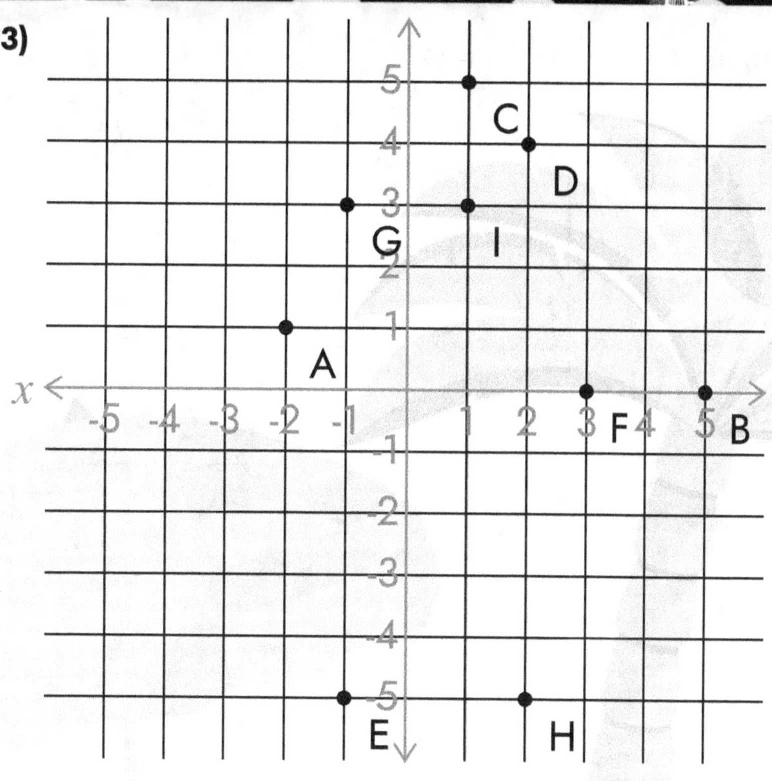

A = _____   B = _____   C = _____

D = _____   E = _____   F = _____

G = _____   H = _____   I = _____

Area and Perimeter

1)

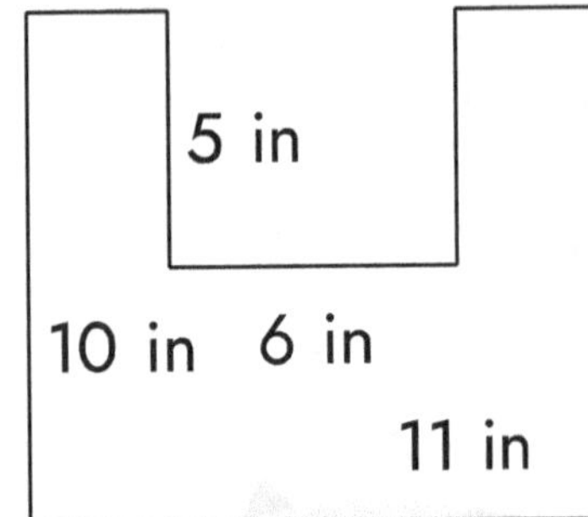

2)

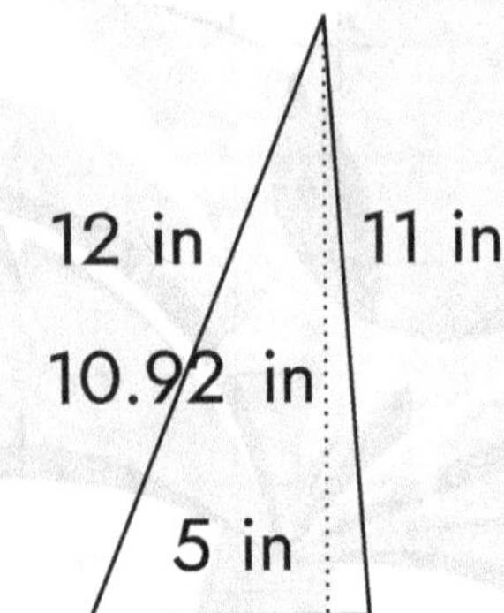

3)

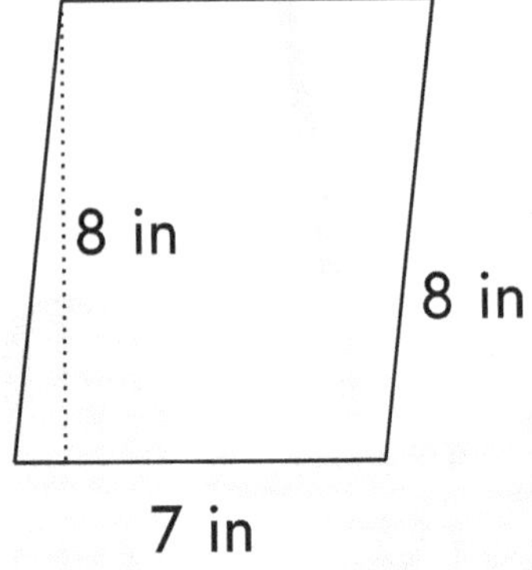

4)

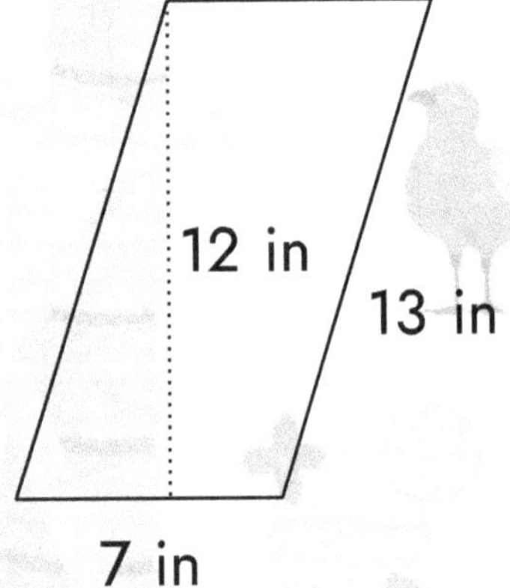

5)

3 in
6 in 2 in
6 in

6)

8 in
9 in
5 in

7)

17 in
17 in
14.722 in
17 in

8)

7 in
5 in
4.00 in
8 in

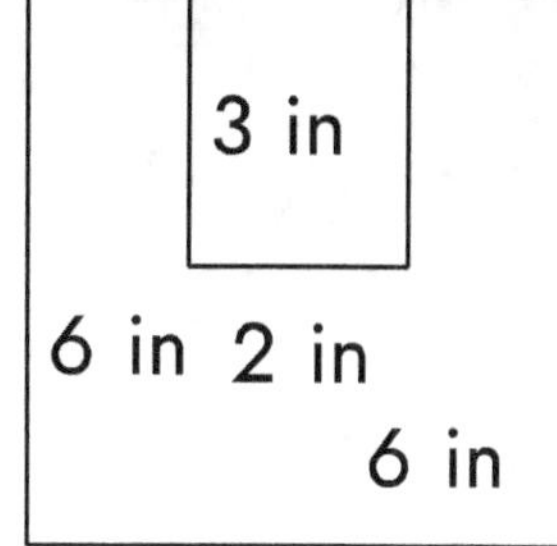

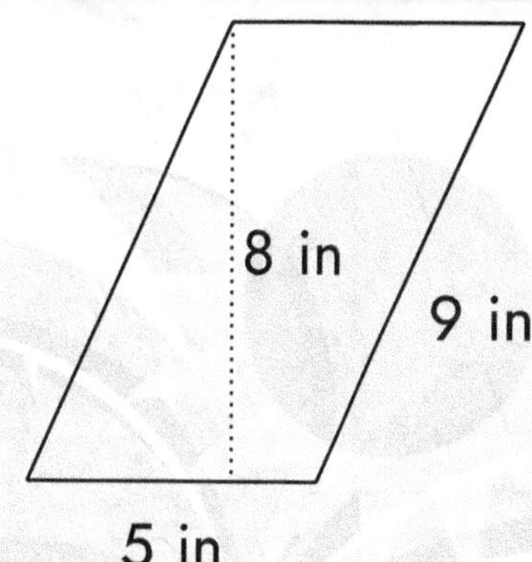

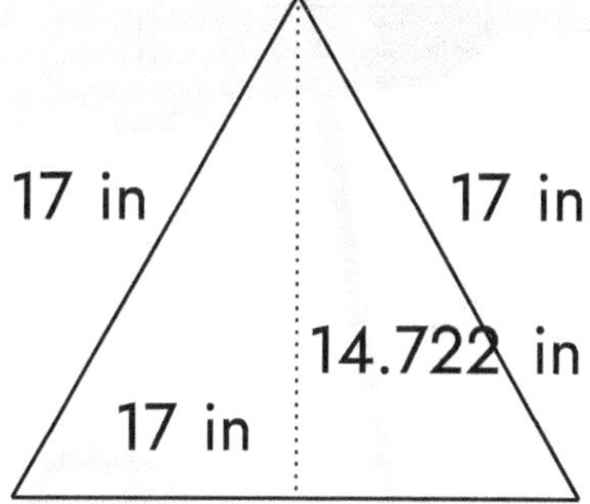

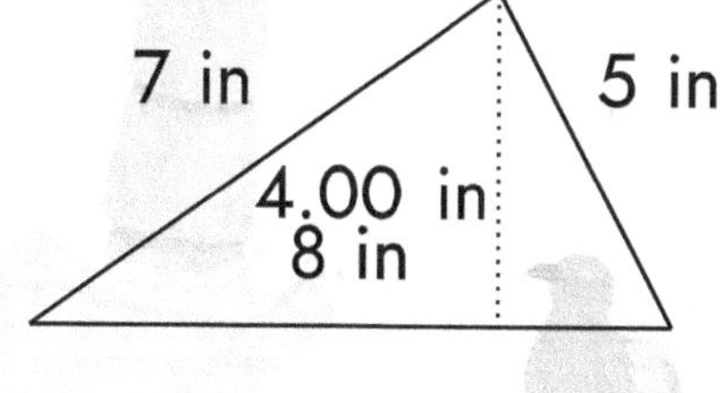

SUMMER MATH WORKBOOK
NAME:
BUILDING ACTIVITIES

9)

12 in
13 in
6 in

10)

7 in
7 in
7 in
6.062 in

11)

5 in
7 in
4.00 in
8 in

12)

9 in
5 in
7 in
5 in

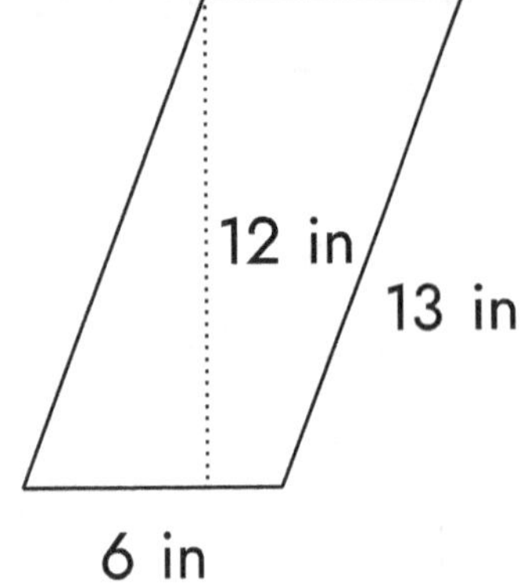

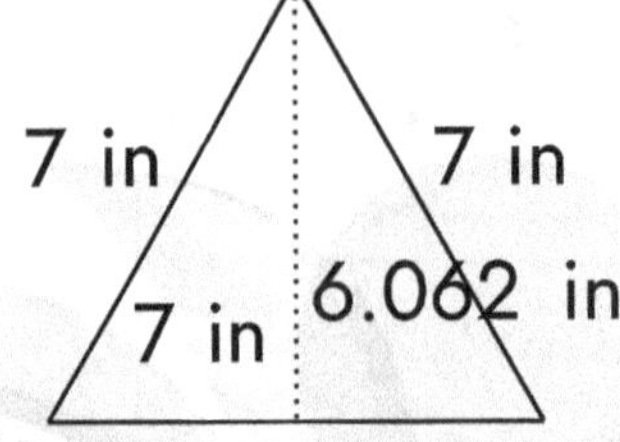

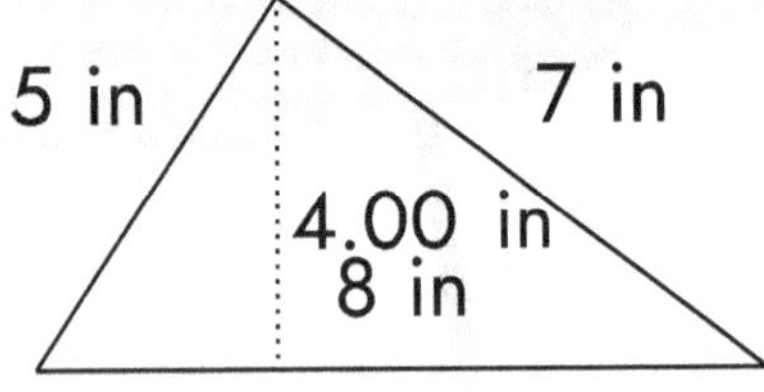

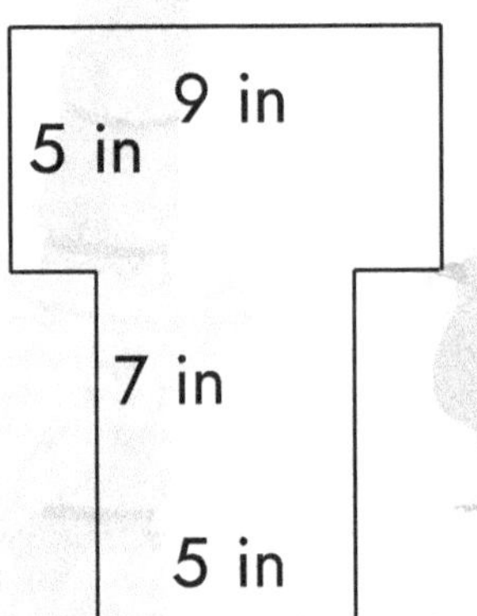

13)

3 in
6 in
5 in
2 in

14)

16 in
11 in
12 in

15)

3 in
3 in
6 in
7 in

16)

17 in
10 in
12 in
5 in

SUMMER MATH WORKBOOK
NAME:
BUILDING ACTIVITIES

17)

24 in
19 in
15 in

18)

19 in
15 in
11 in

19)

11 in
12 in

20)

9 in
15 in
10 in
15 in

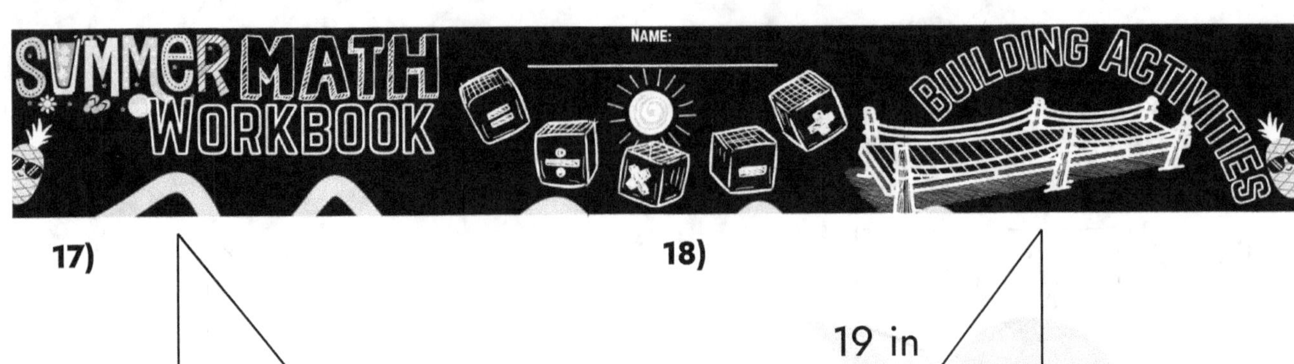

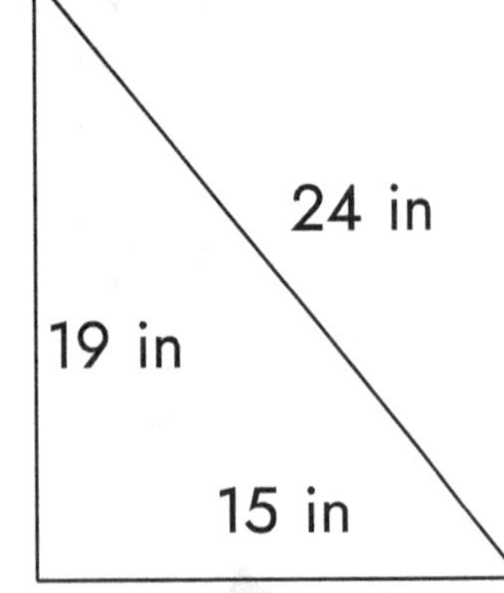

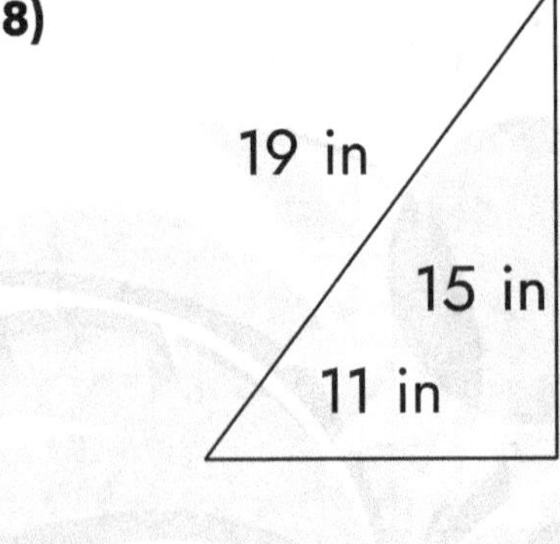

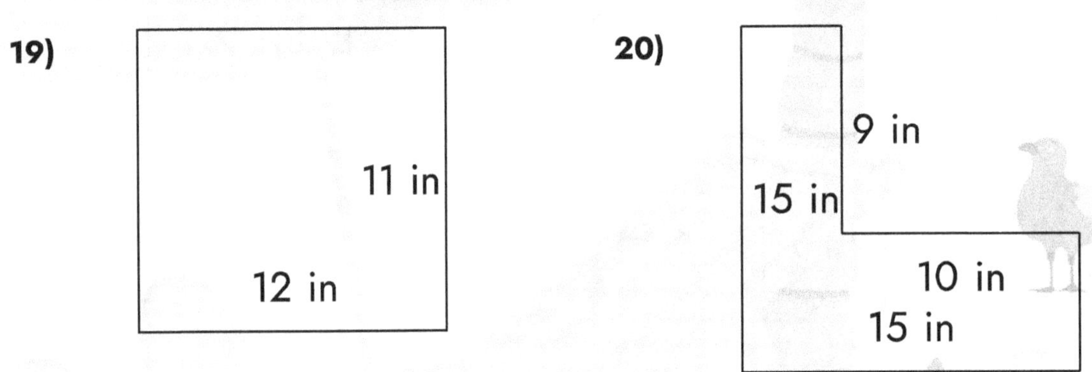

SUMMER MATH WORKBOOK
NAME:
BUILDING ACTIVITIES

21)

16 in
16 in
13.856 in
16 in

22)

9 in
3 in
10 in
4 in

23)

9 in
16 in
8 in
13 in

24)

22 in
16 in
15 in

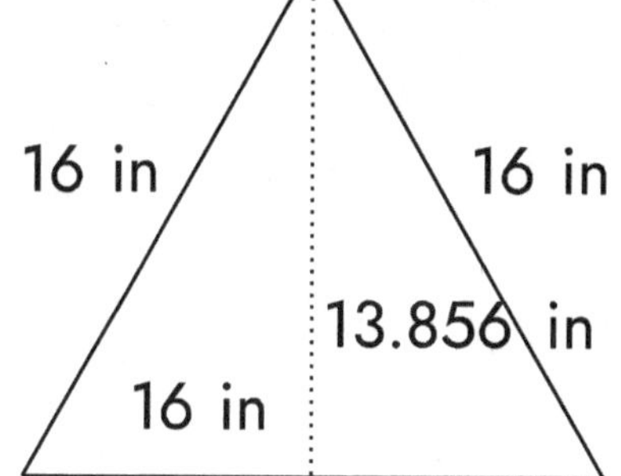

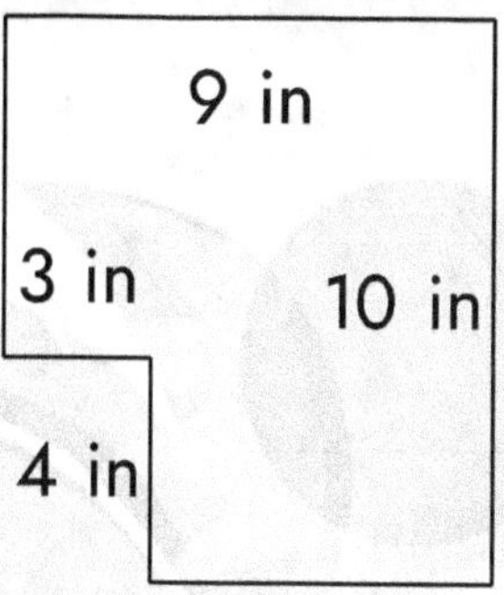

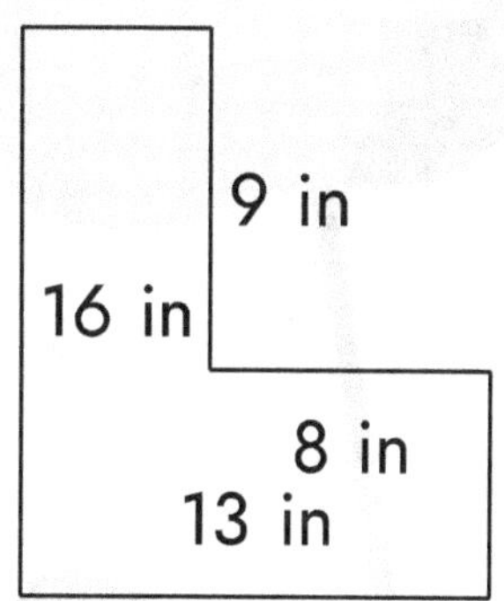

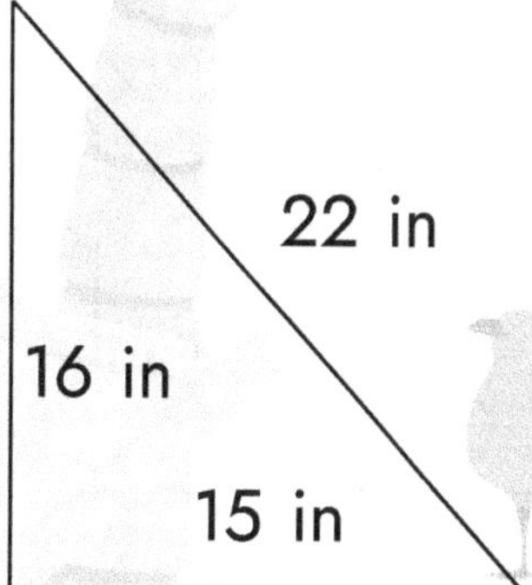

25)

12 in
14 in
10 in

26)

8 in
8 in
7.64 in
3 in

27)

16 in
11 in
12 in

28)

14 in
14 in
12.87 in
11 in

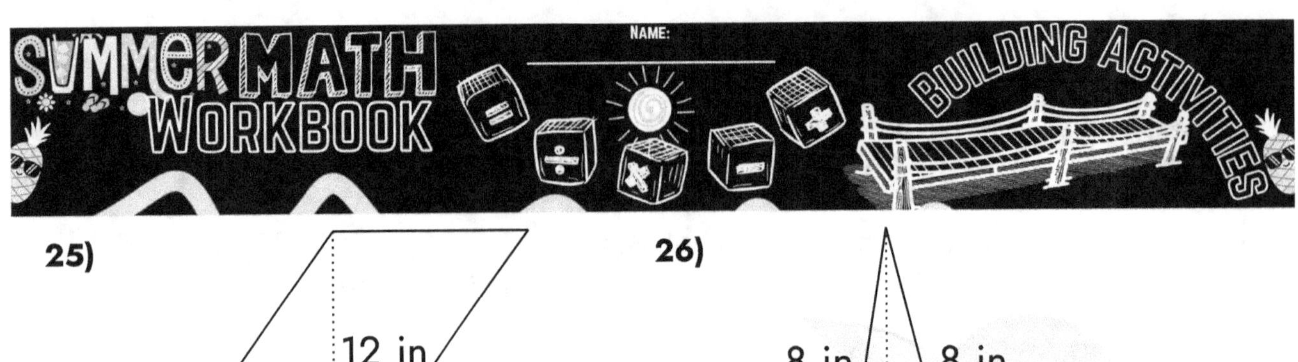

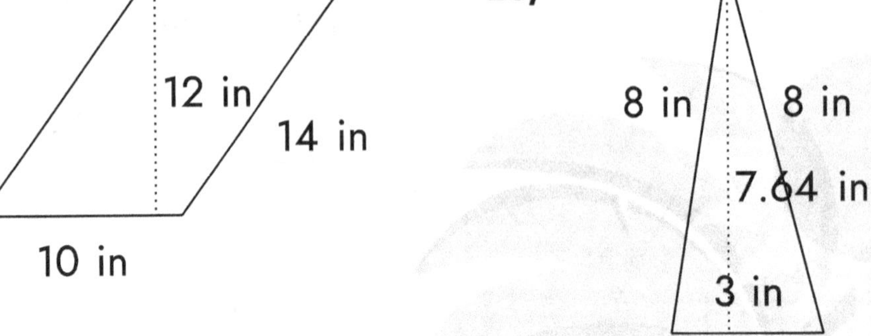

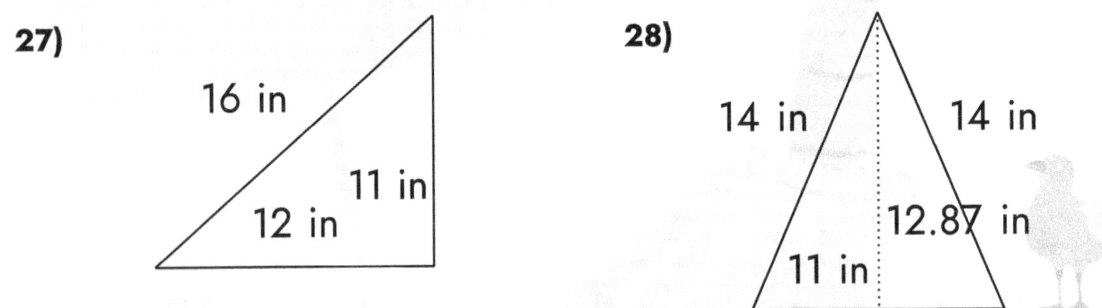

Pythagorean Theorem

Find the length of the side.

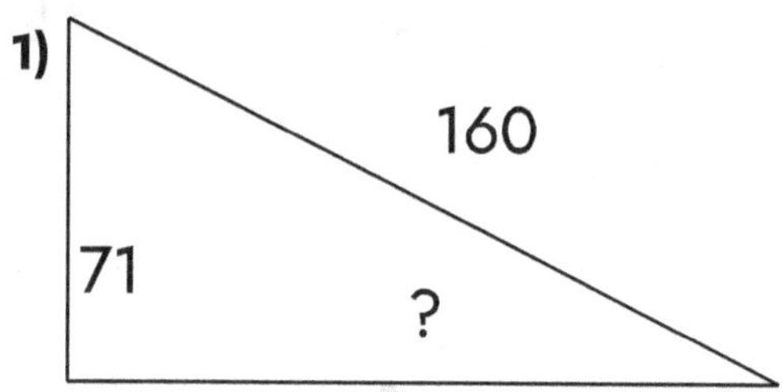

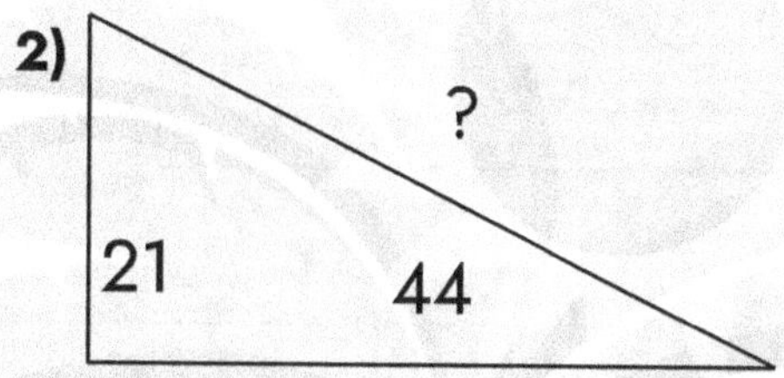

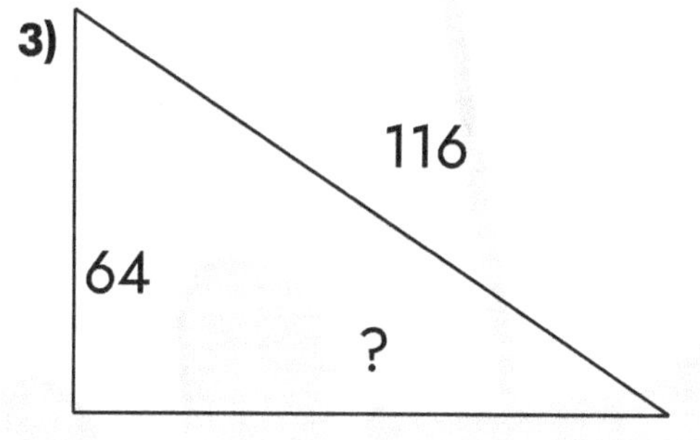

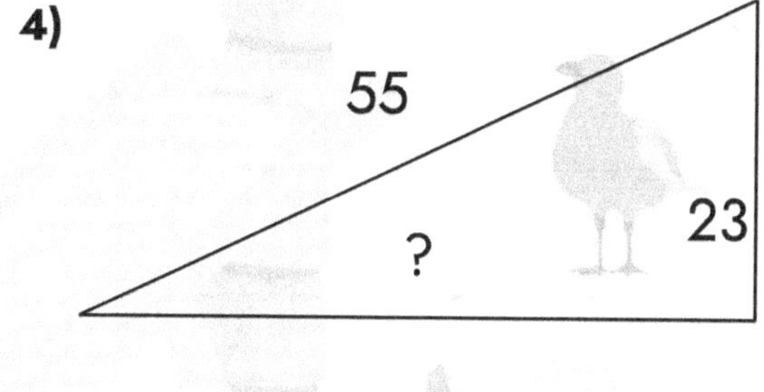

SUMMER MATH WORKBOOK
NAME:
BUILDING ACTIVITIES

5)

?
95
46

6)

?
104
38

____

7)

80
?
69

____

8)

193
?
164

____

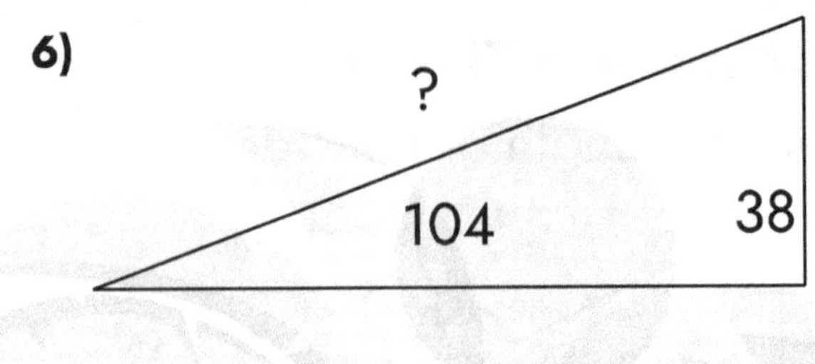

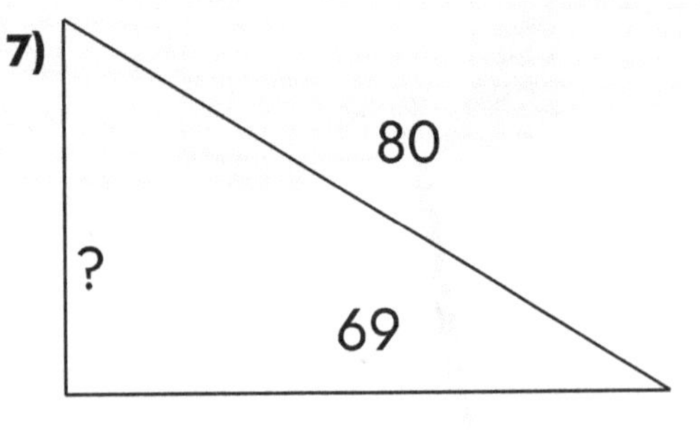

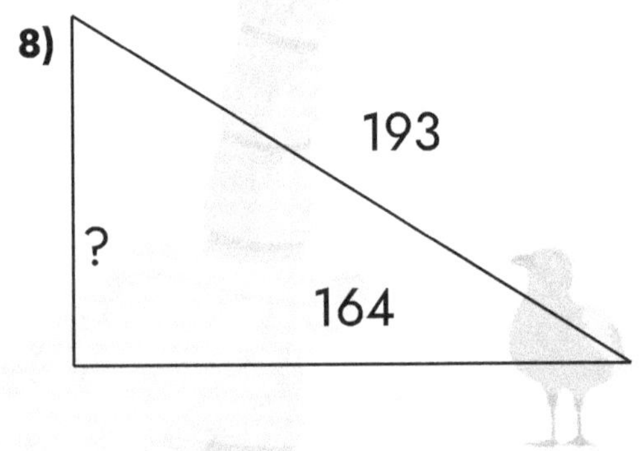

SUMMER MATH WORKBOOK
NAME:
BUILDING ACTIVITIES

9)

66
38
?

____

10)

76
?
67

____

11)

?
62
122

____

12)

?
50
28

____

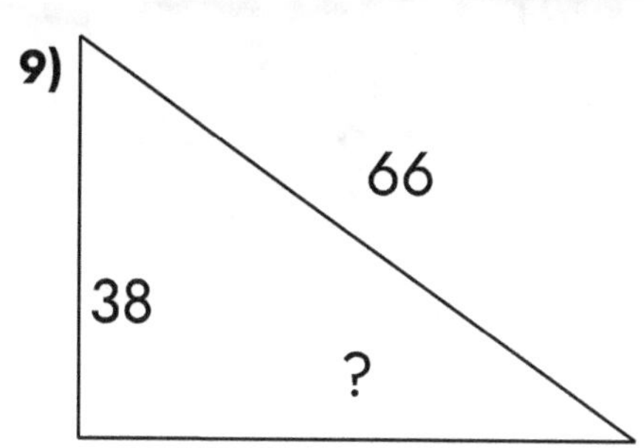

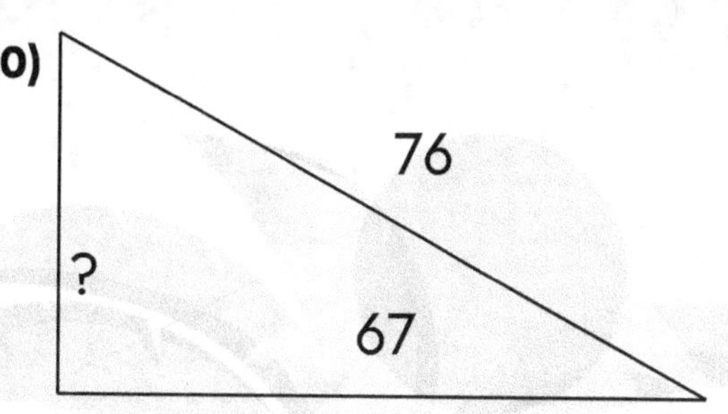

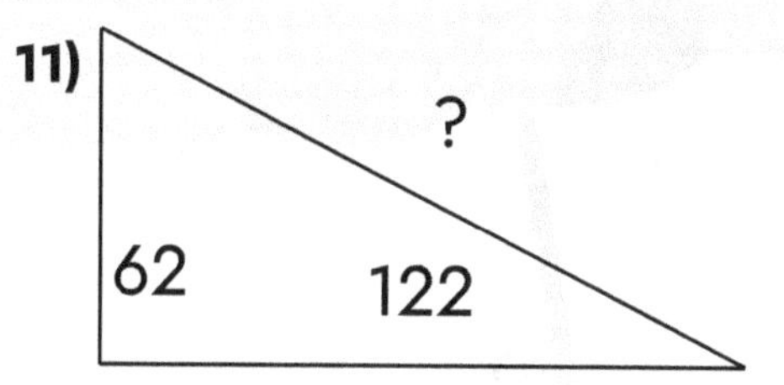

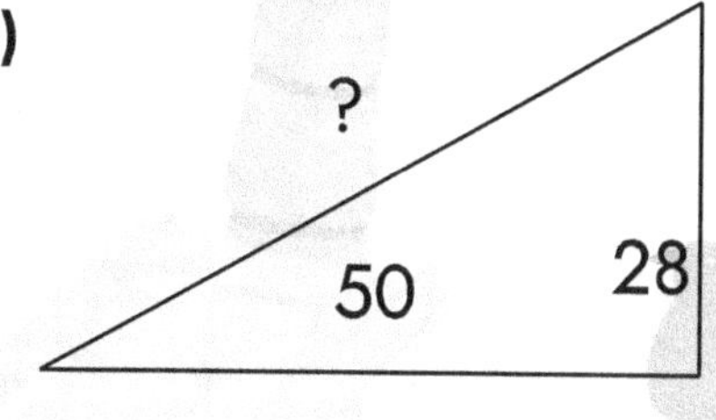

13)

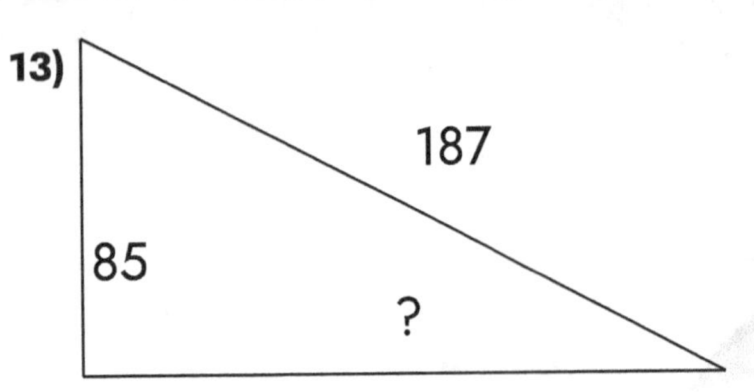

____

14)

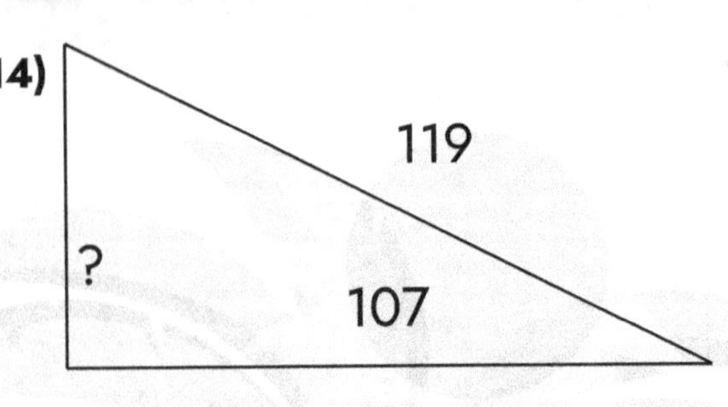

____

15)

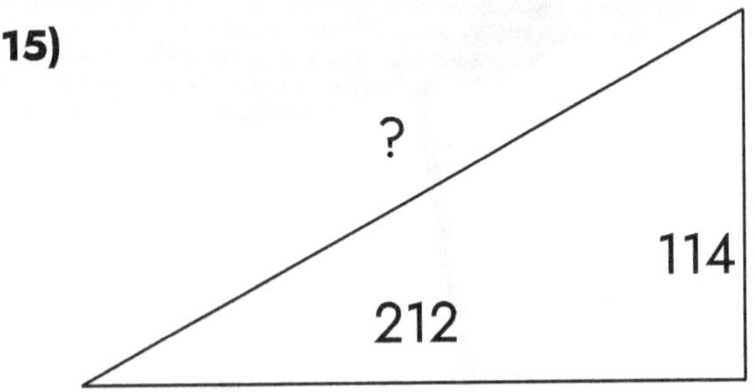

____

16)

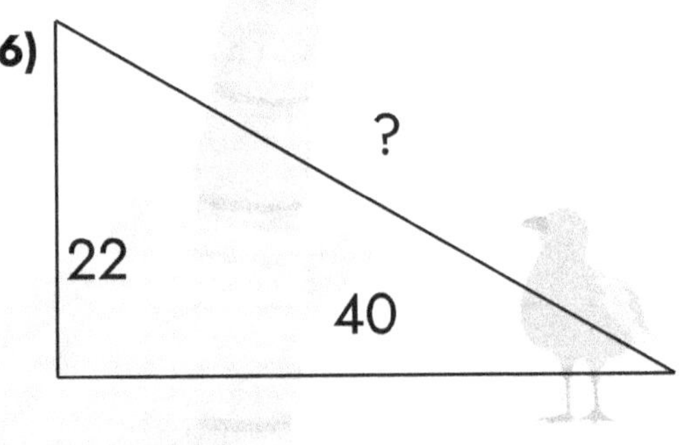

____

17)

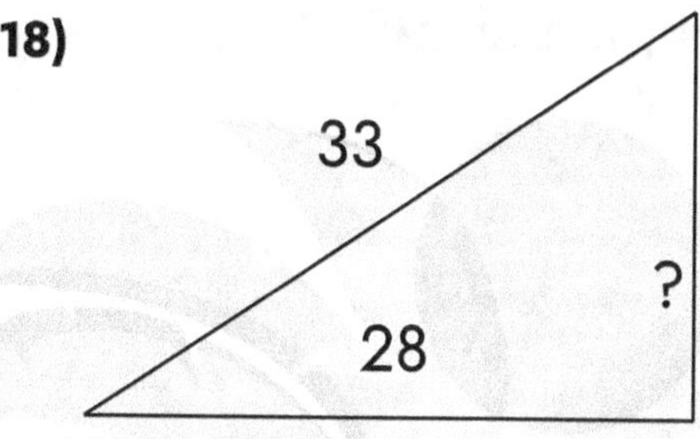

____

18)

____

19)

____

20)

____

Volume and Surface Area

1)

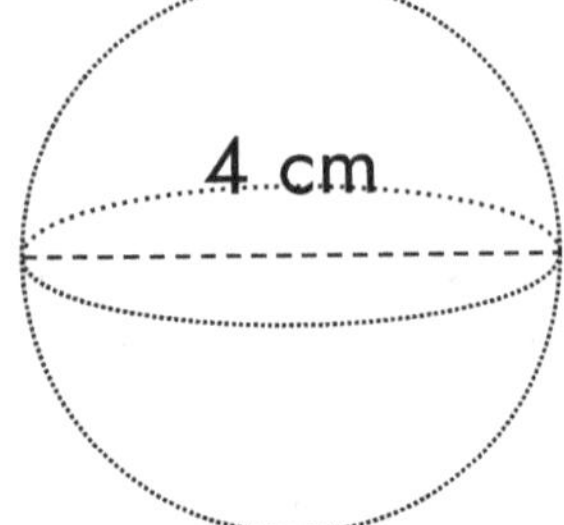

2)

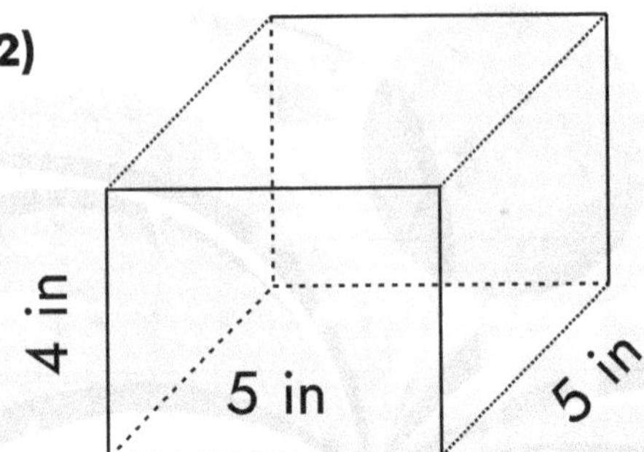

3)

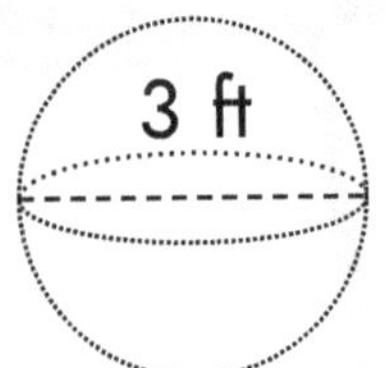

4)

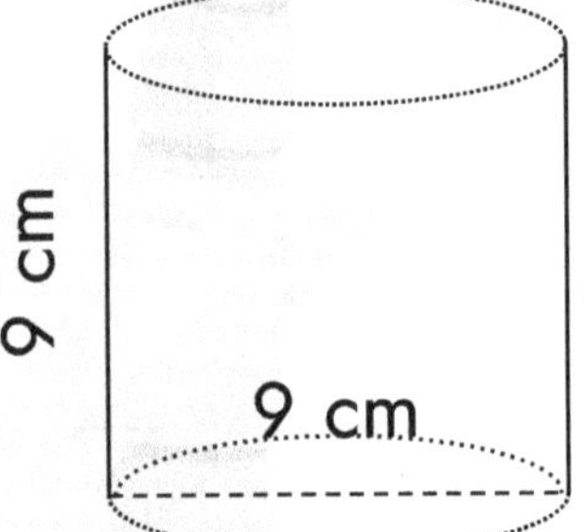

5)

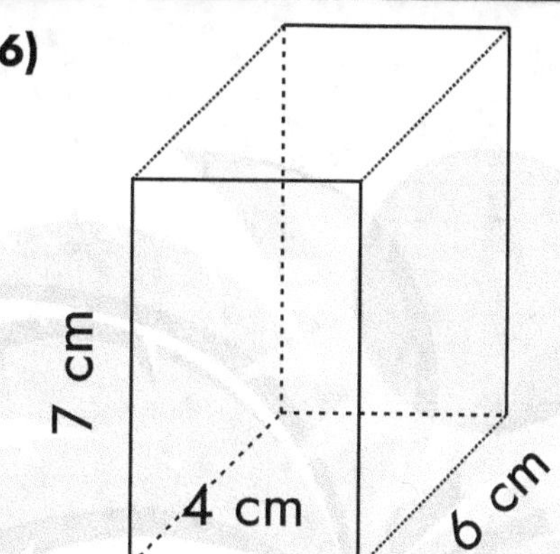

6)

7)

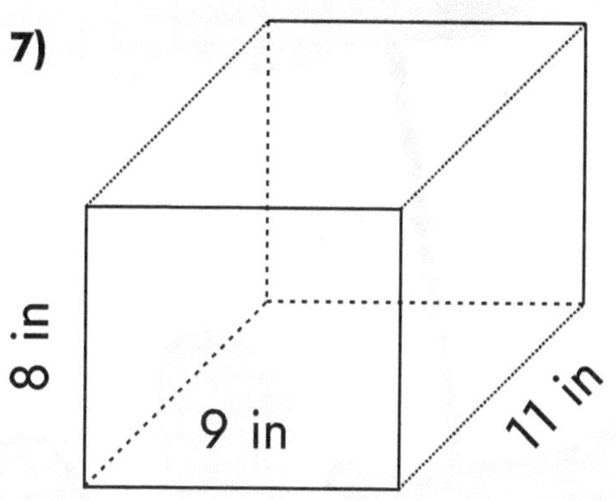

8)

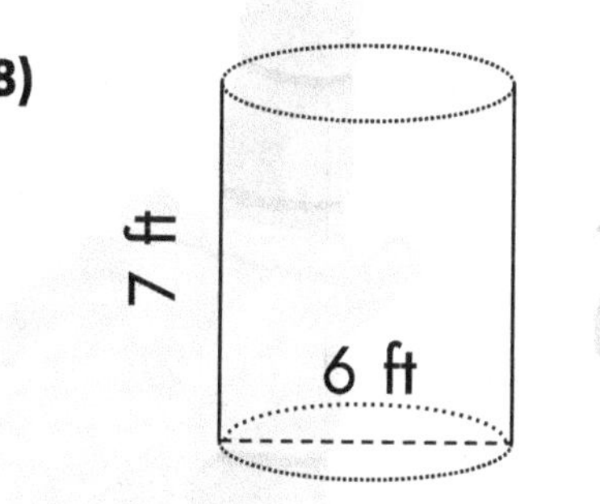

9)

2 cm

10)

5 cm

7 cm

6 cm

11)

7 cm

9 cm

6 cm

12)

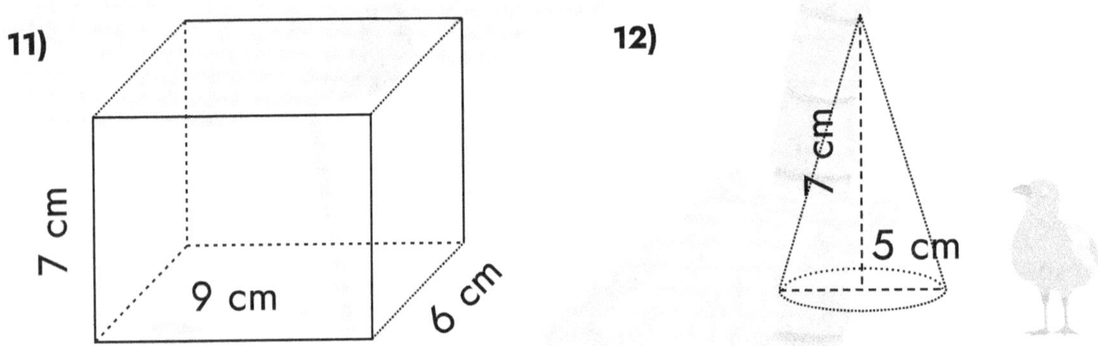

7 cm

5 cm

SUMMER MATH WORKBOOK
NAME:
BUILDING ACTIVITIES

13)

2 in
3 in
3 in

14)

5 cm
8 cm

15)

3 cm
2 cm
3 cm

16)

2 in
3 in
2 in

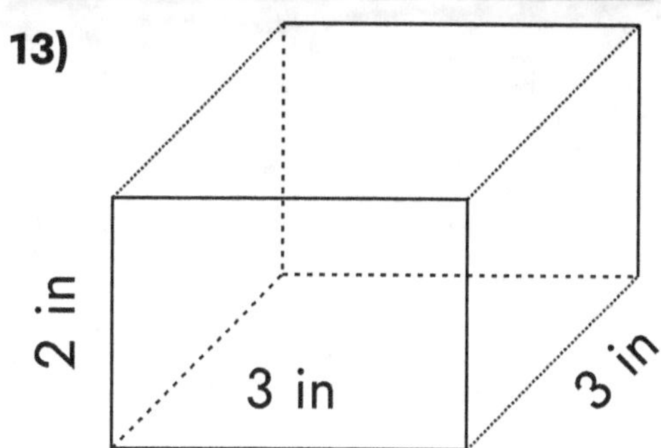

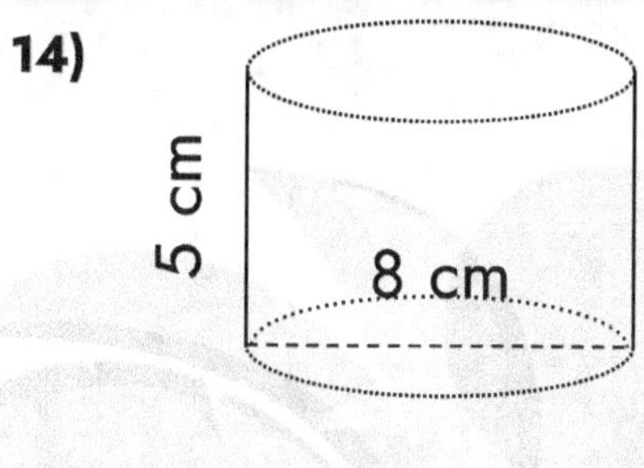

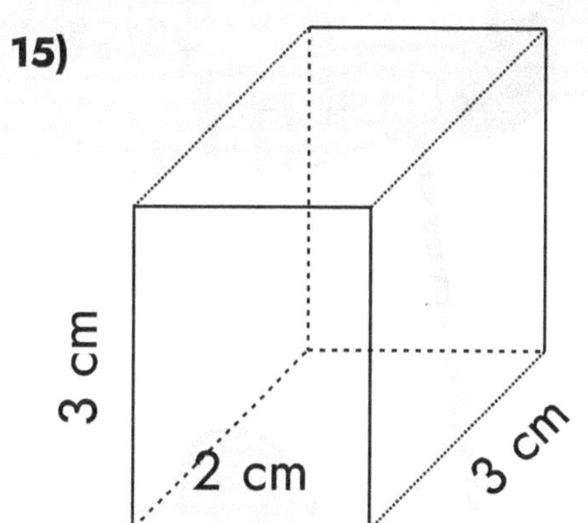

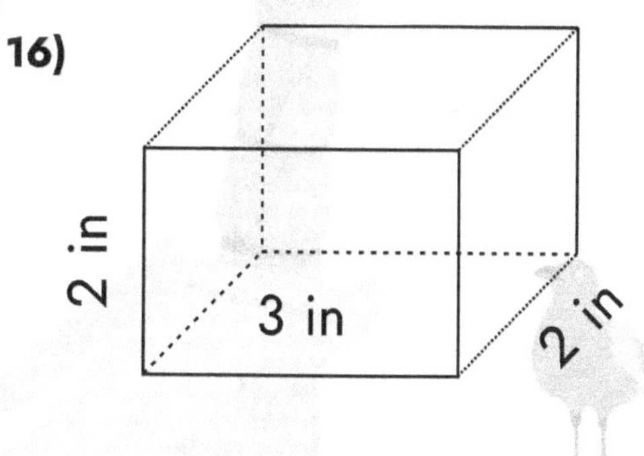

17)

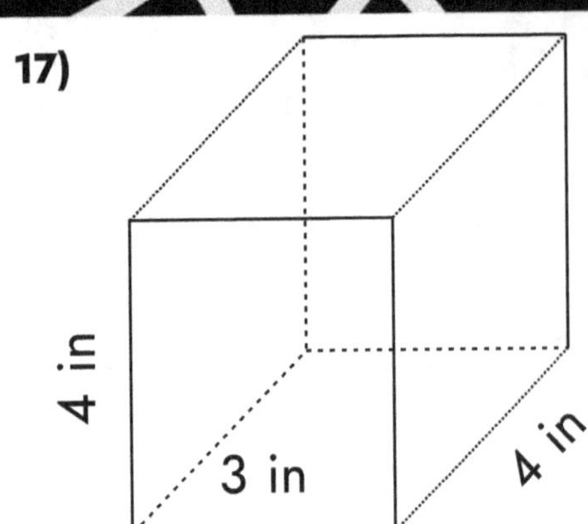

18)

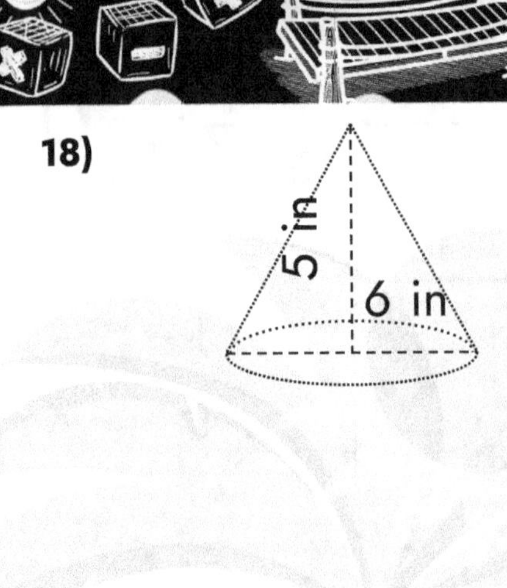

19)

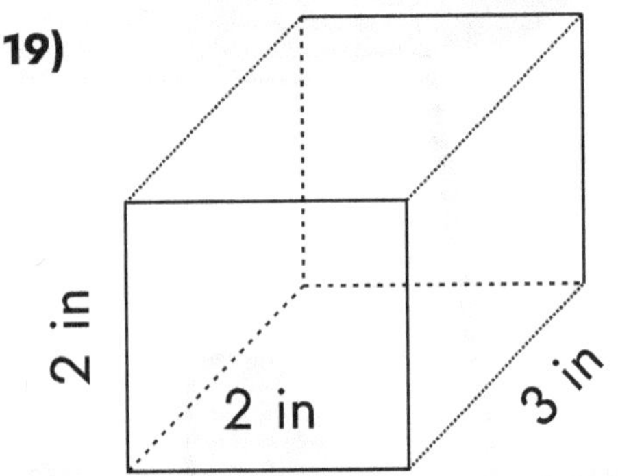

20)

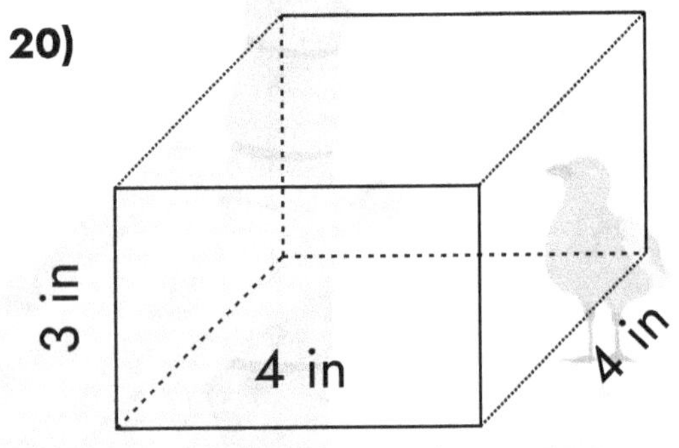

21)

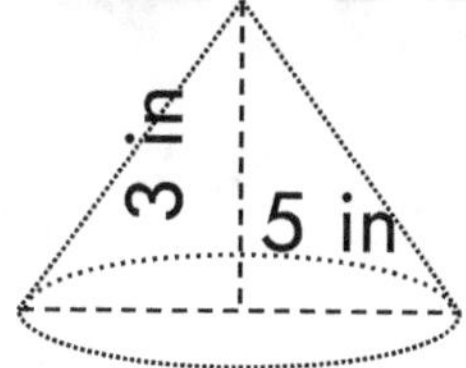

22)

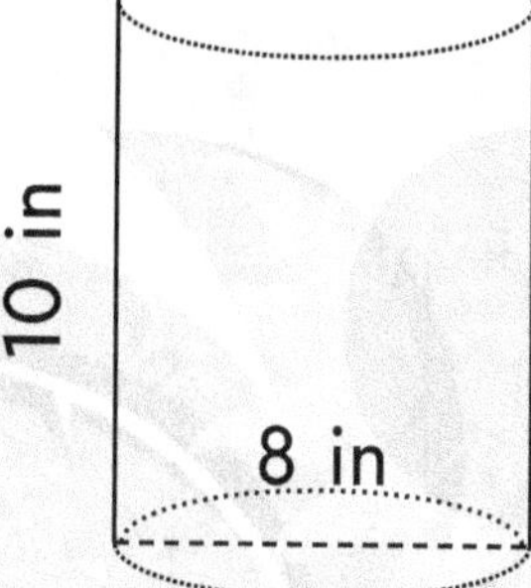

23)

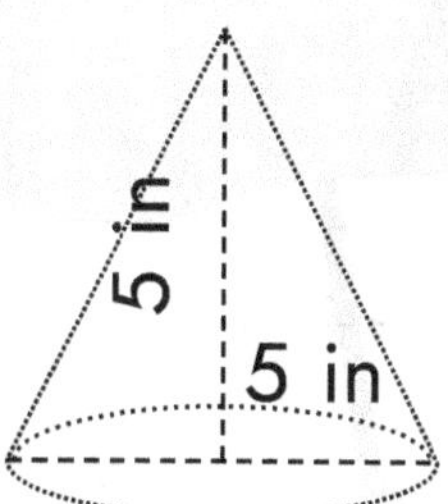

24)

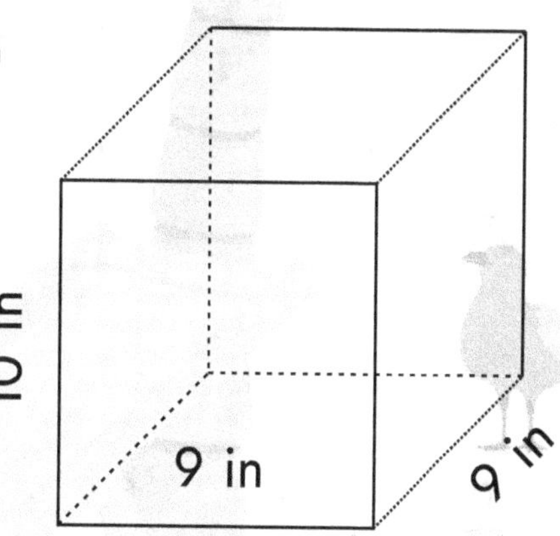

SUMMER MATH WORKBOOK
NAME:
BUILDING ACTIVITIES

25)

5 in
7 in
9 in

26)

4 in
4 in
5 in

27)

5 ft
6 ft
6 ft

28)

3 in
5 in
7 in

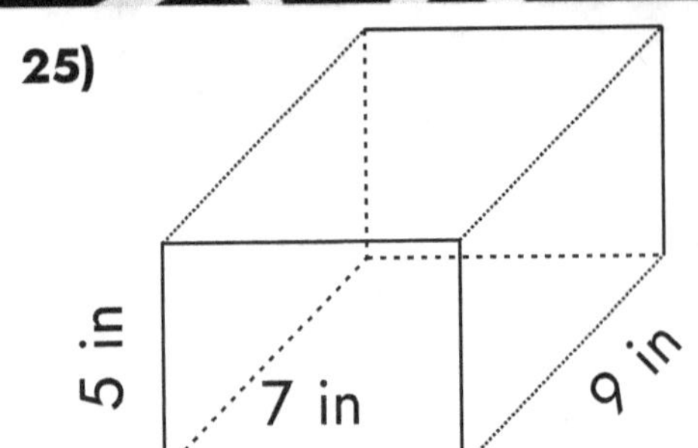

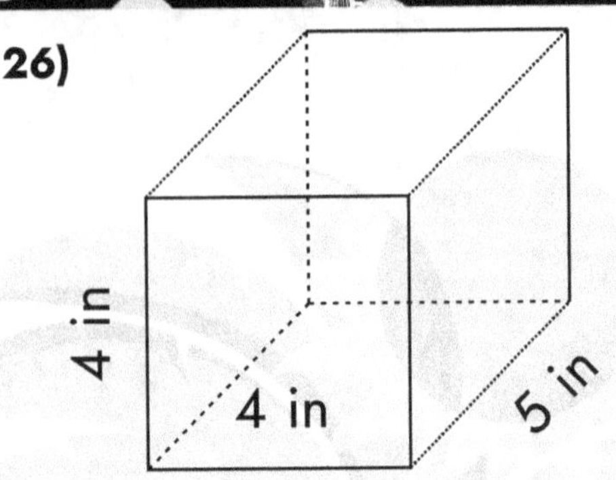

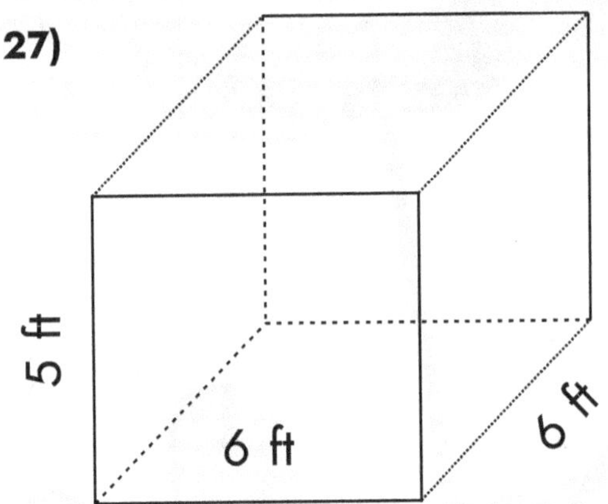

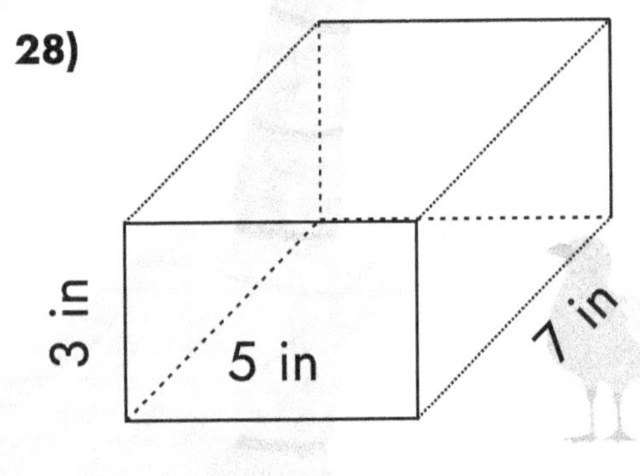

Mean, Median, Mode, and Range

Find the Mean, Median, Mode and Range of the following sets of data.

1) 31, 76, 51, 8, 83, 59

Mean = _____   Median = _____

Mode = _____   Range = _____

2) 77, 34, 90, 72, 72, 3

Mean = _____   Median = _____

Mode = _____   Range = _____

3) 24, 58, 74, 24, 30, 6

Mean = _____   Median = _____

Mode = _____   Range = _____

4) 1, 46, 95, 58, 64, 4

Mean = ______   Median = ____

Mode = ______   Range = ____

5) 95, 15, 12, 15, 74, 35, 23

Mean = ______   Median = ____

Mode = ______   Range = ____

6) 17, 23, 60, 51, 40, 9

Mean = ______   Median = ____

Mode = ______   Range = ____

7) 70, 27, 3, 60, 17, 57, 91

Mean = ______   Median = ____

Mode = ______   Range = ____

8) 31, 62, 77, 93, 17, 92, 89

Mean = _______   Median = _______

Mode = _______   Range = _______

9) 51, 29, 21, 29, 73, 12

Mean = _______   Median = _______

Mode = _______   Range = _______

10) 48, 13, 68, 47, 63, 60, 56

Mean = _______   Median = _______

Mode = _______   Range = _______

11) 50, 56, 79, 63, 7, 35, 16

Mean = _______   Median = _______

Mode = _______   Range = _______

12) 59, 79, 98, 86, 79, 2, 72

Mean = ______ Median = ____

Mode = ______ Range = ____

13) 72, 33, 37, 18, 97, 81

Mean = ______ Median = ____

Mode = ______ Range = ____

14) 45, 71, 87, 2, 32, 78, 28

Mean = ____ Median = ____

Mode = ____ Range = ____

15) 60, 58, 58, 55, 96, 57, 1

Mean = ____ Median = ____

Mode = ____ Range = ____

16) 42, 75, 82, 15, 86, 82

Mean = _______   Median = _______

Mode = _______   Range = _______

17) 76, 31, 72, 31, 35, 50

Mean = _______   Median = _______

Mode = _______   Range = _______

18) 72, 40, 75, 79, 32, 30

Mean = _______   Median = _______

Mode = _______   Range = _______

19) 66, 78, 11, 78, 68, 77, 32

Mean = _______   Median = _______

Mode = _______   Range = _______

ANSWERS

Page 1: Order of Operations (PEMDAS)

1. 27 **2.** 10 **3.** 12 **4.** 19 **5.** 13 **6.** 26 **7.** 19 **8.** 13 **9.** 9

10. 18 **11.** 13 **12.** 21 **13.** 22 **14.** 25 **15.** 17 **16.** 22 **17.** 21 **18.** 21

19. 14 **20.** 16 **21.** 32 **22.** 33 **23.** 16 **24.** 19 **25.** 24 **26.** 21 **27.** 14

28. 22 **29.** 22 **30.** 22 **31.** 24 **32.** 27 **33.** 14 **34.** 24 **35.** 23 **36.** 18

37. 12 **38.** 20

Page 5: Evaluate Expressions

1. 4 **2.** 4 **3.** 9 **4.** 4 **5.** 1 **6.** 8 **7.** 3 **8.** 2 **9.** 7 **10.** 2 **11.** 1

12. 6 **13.** 2 **14.** 6 **15.** 2 **16.** 4 **17.** 6 **18.** 9 **19.** 7 **20.** 8 **21.** 7 **22.** 2

23. 6 **24.** 2 **25.** 7 **26.** 5 **27.** 7 **28.** 1

Page 12: Solving Inequalities

1. $y < 7$ **2.** $x \leq 2/5$ **3.** $k \leq -5$ **4.** $k < -3$ **5.** $m \geq 4/3$

6. $y \geq -11$ **7.** $k > -8$ **8.** $y > -16$ **9.** $m \geq -10$ **10.** $x > 6$

11. $x > -7$ **12.** $k \leq 48$ **13.** $m \geq 16$ **14.** $k > -1$ **15.** $z < 4$

16. $k \geq 5$ **17.** $m > 2$ **18.** $x < -2$ **19.** $x \leq -42$ **20.** $y > -13$

21. $m < -12$ **22.** $m \geq -3/4$ **23.** $y \geq -3$ **24.** $x < 13$ **25.** $z \leq 0$

26. $k \leq -4$ **27.** $k > 27$ **28.** $m \leq -6$

Page 19: Find Numbers

1. 7, 30 **2.** 8 **3.** 5, 25 **4.** 7, 10 **5.** 16 **6.** -7, 1 **7.** 3

8. 6, 3 **9.** 10 **10.** 18 **11.** 8 **12.** 2 **13.** 2, 4 **14.** 0

15. 28 **16.** 6 **17.** 5 **18.** 1 **19.** 0, 0 **20.** 6, 60 **21.** 12, 8

22. 3 **23.** 3, 30

Page 24: Solving Equations: (One Side)

1. $k = 3$ **2.** $x = 8$ **3.** $z = 2$ **4.** $z = 4$ **5.** $z = 12$

6. $z = 4$ **7.** $x = 6$ **8.** $z = 16$ **9.** $z = 16$ **10.** $y = 1$

11. $y = 19$ **12.** $k = 1$ **13.** $m = 320$ **14.** $z = 17$ **15.** $y = 10$

16. $x = 19$ **17.** $k = 7$ **18.** $y = 6$ **19.** $x = 7$ **20.** $x = 20$

21. $z = 19$ **22.** $y = 2$ **23.** $m = 4$ **24.** $y = 8$ **25.** $x = 247$

26. $y = 1$ **27.** $y = 9$ **28.** $z = 14$

Page 27: Solving Equations (Two Sides)

1. $k = 4$ **2.** $x = 5$ **3.** $x = 8$ **4.** $x = 3$ **5.** $k = 3$ **6.** $x = 5$ **7.** $m = 6$

8. $k = 7$ **9.** $x = 3$ **10.** $m = 3$ **11.** $k = 4$ **12.** $k = 8$ **13.** $k = 6$ **14.** $x = 1$

15. $m = 5$ **16.** $m = 8$ **17.** $x = 5$ **18.** $x = 4$ **19.** $z = 1$ **20.** $x = 9$ **21.** $x = 5$

22. $x = 1$ **23.** $z = 2$ **24.** $m = 3$ **25.** $x = 6$ **26.** $m = 2$ **27.** $m = 1$ **28.** $x = 9$

29. $x = 7$

Page 33: Proportional Relationship

1. 112 **2.** 160 **3.** 5 **4.** 117 **5.** 11 **6.** 12 **7.** 14 **8.** 4 **9.** 48

10. 40 **11.** 9 **12.** 18 **13.** 10 **14.** 112 **15.** 12 **16.** 78 **17.** 63 **18.** 9

19. 19 **20.** 15

Page 35: Percentage

1. 300 **2.** 160 **3.** 450 **4.** 1800 **5.** 75% **6.** 30% **7.** 30

8. 15% **9.** 300 **10.** 35 **11.** 160 **12.** 10% **13.** 12 **14.** 25%

15. 5%   **16.** 8   **17.** 100   **18.** 800   **19.** 280   **20.** 200%   **21.** 100

22. 8   **23.** 500   **24.** 50%   **25.** 40   **26.** 60   **27.** 54   **28.** 100

29. 9   **30.** 90   **31.** 8%   **32.** 4%   **33.** 900   **34.** 14   **35.** 140

36. 90%

Page 38:

1. 0.8%   **2.** 0.305   **3.** 4.8%   **4.** 227   **5.** 61   **6.** 95.241

7. 1.976   **8.** 31.9%   **9.** 96   **10.** 285   **11.** 6.6%   **12.** 2

13. 8.3%   **14.** 22.4%   **15.** 6   **16.** 2.775   **17.** 235   **18.** 994

19. 0.7%   **20.** 4.324   **21.** 0.003   **22.** 15.7%   **23.** 9.0%   **24.** 3.576

25. 28.213   **26.** 0.4%   **27.** 0.36   **28.** 0.5%   **29.** 2.718   **30.** 53

31. 98   **32.** 0.042   **33.** 0.084   **34.** 0.8%   **35.** 0.57   **36.** 4.8%

37. 0.22   **38.** 5

Page 42:   Ratio Conversions

1.

	Ratio	Fraction	Percent	Decimal
a.	4:17	4/17	23.5%	0.235
b.	4:14	4/14	28.6%	0.286
c.	1:1	1/1	100%	1
d.	1:5	1/5	20%	0.2
e.	3:9	3/9	33.3%	0.333
f.	6:15	6/15	40%	0.4
g.	1:18	1/18	5.6%	0.056
h.	5:17	5/17	29.4%	0.294
i.	12:20	12/20	60%	0.6
j.	1:6	1/6	16.7%	0.167
k.	1:20	1/20	5%	0.05
l.	1:13	1/13	7.7%	0.077
m.	2:5	2/5	40%	0.4
n.	1:3	1/3	33.3%	0.333
o.	2:15	2/15	13.3%	0.133

2.

	Ratio	Fraction	Percent	Decimal
a.	5:7	5/7	71.4%	0.714
b.	2:2	2/2	100%	1
c.	9:11	9/11	81.8%	0.818
d.	6:20	6/20	30%	0.3
e.	4:5	4/5	80%	0.8
f.	6:7	6/7	85.7%	0.857
g.	4:12	4/12	33.3%	0.333
h.	8:13	8/13	61.5%	0.615
i.	1:5	1/5	20%	0.2
j.	18:20	18/20	90%	0.9
k.	2:7	2/7	28.6%	0.286
l.	9:13	9/13	69.2%	0.692
m.	1:2	1/2	50%	0.5
n.	16:19	16/19	84.2%	0.842
o.	2:17	2/17	11.8%	0.118

3.

	Ratio	Fraction	Percent	Decimal
a.	1:4	1/4	25%	0.25
b.	8:11	8/11	72.7%	0.727
c.	3:4	3/4	75%	0.75
d.	1:16	1/16	6.2%	0.062
e.	7:15	7/15	46.7%	0.467
f.	12:14	12/14	85.7%	0.857
g.	2:11	2/11	18.2%	0.182
h.	4:17	4/17	23.5%	0.235
i.	3:14	3/14	21.4%	0.214
j.	6:14	6/14	42.9%	0.429
k.	9:10	9/10	90%	0.9
l.	10:13	10/13	76.9%	0.769
m.	9:14	9/14	64.3%	0.643
n.	15:19	15/19	78.9%	0.789
o.	6:10	6/10	60%	0.6

Page 45:   Cartesian Coordinates

1.
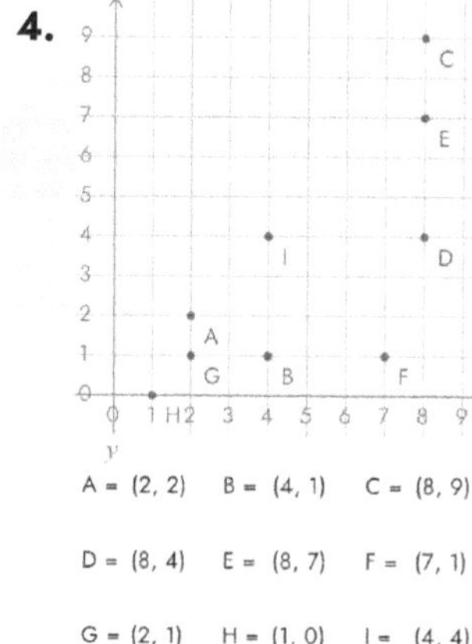

A = (4, 1)   B = (5, 3)   C = (6, 5)

D = (3, 2)   E = (7, 4)   F = (8, 8)

G = (5, 7)   H = (1, 4)   I = (6, 3)

2.
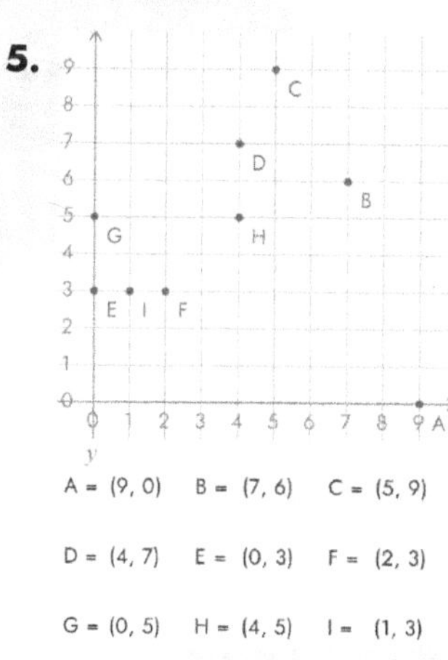

A = (9, 5)   B = (0, 4)   C = (0, 1)

D = (4, 6)   E = (5, 8)   F = (3, 9)

G = (6, 6)   H = (6, 3)   I = (5, 1)

3.

A = (0, 1)   B = (3, 8)   C = (7, 4)

D = (9, 1)   E = (7, 6)   F = (5, 2)

G = (6, 0)   H = (9, 0)   I = (2, 0)

4.

A = (2, 2)   B = (4, 1)   C = (8, 9)

D = (8, 4)   E = (8, 7)   F = (7, 1)

G = (2, 1)   H = (1, 0)   I = (4, 4)

5.

A = (9, 0)   B = (7, 6)   C = (5, 9)

D = (4, 7)   E = (0, 3)   F = (2, 3)

G = (0, 5)   H = (4, 5)   I = (1, 3)

Page 50:   Cartesian Coordinates

1. 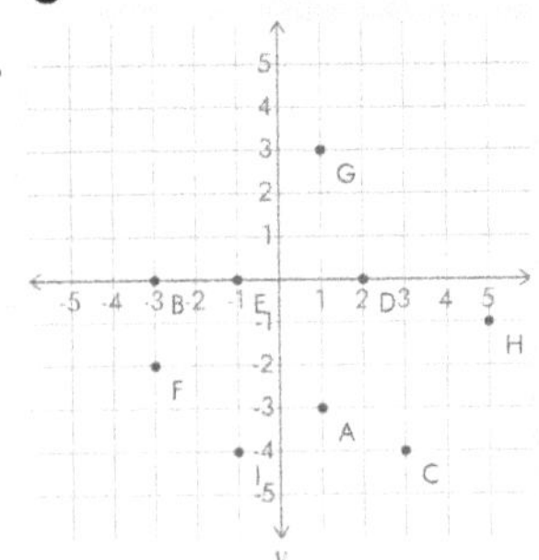

A = (6, 8)   B = (3, 4)   C = (0, 2)

D = (5, 1)   E = (3, 6)   F = (4, 4)

G = (0, 5)   H = (5, 4)   I = (1, 2)

2. 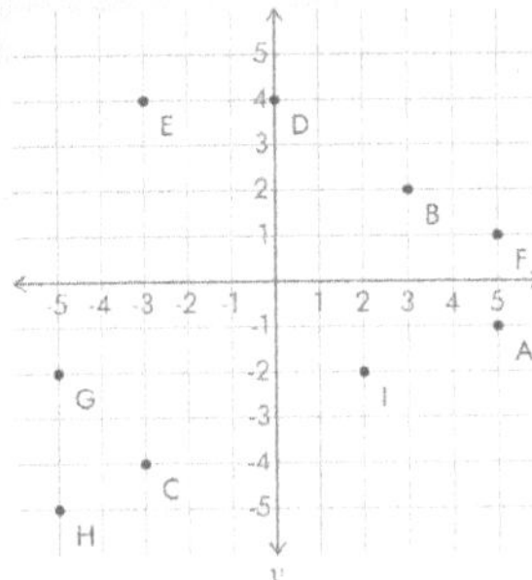

A = (2, 5)   B = (6, 5)   C = (7, 0)

D = (8, 4)   E = (1, 5)   F = (7, 2)

G = (7, 7)   H = (0, 8)   I = (3, 6)

3. 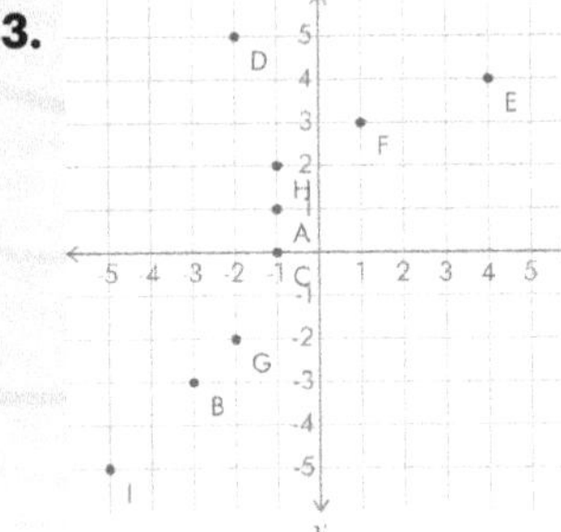

A = (0, 3)   B = (5, 5)   C = (1, 9)

D = (4, 1)   E = (9, 6)   F = (3, 5)

G = (2, 7)   H = (4, 3)   I = (0, 0)

Page 53:   Cartesian Coordinates With Four Quadrants

1.

A = (1, -3)   B = (-3, 0)   C = (3, -4)

D = (2, 0)   E = (-1, 0)   F = (-3, -2)

G = (1, 3)   H = (5, -1)   I = (-1, -4)

2.

A = (5, -1)   B = (3, 2)   C = (-3, -4)

D = (0, 4)   E = (-3, 4)   F = (5, 1)

G = (-5, -2)   H = (-5, -5)   I = (2, -2)

3.

A = (-1, 1)   B = (-3, -3)   C = (-1, 0)

D = (-2, 5)   E = (4, 4)   F = (1, 3)

G = (-2, -2)   H = (-1, 2)   I = (-5, -5)

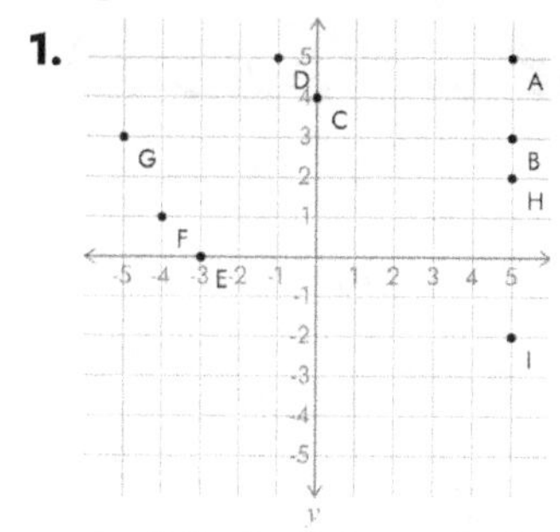
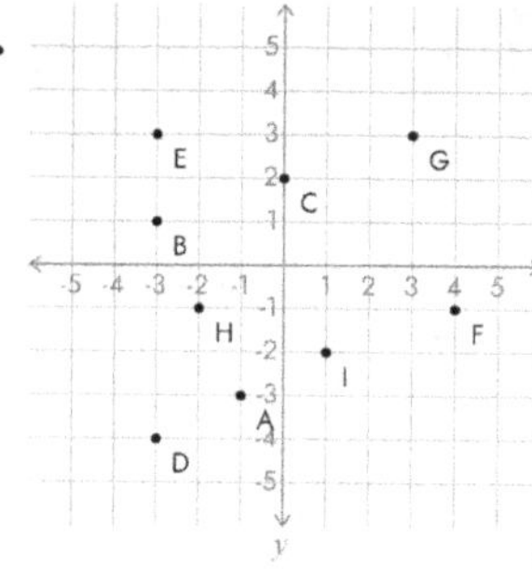
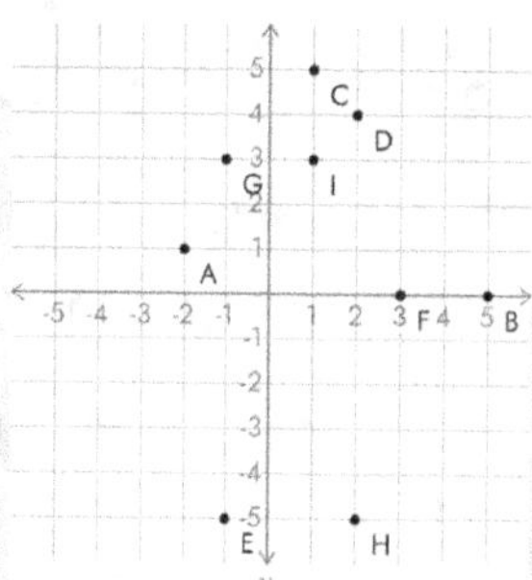

Page 56: Cartesian Coordinates With Four Quadrants

1.

A = (5, 5)   B = (5, 3)   C = (0, 4)

D = (-1, 5)   E = (-3, 0)   F = (-4, 1)

G = (-5, 3)   H = (5, 2)   I = (5, -2)

2.

A = (-1, -3)   B = (-3, 1)   C = (0, 2)

D = (-3, -4)   E = (-3, 3)   F = (4, -1)

G = (3, 3)   H = (-2, -1)   I = (1, -2)

3.

A = (-2, 1)   B = (5, 0)   C = (1, 5)

D = (2, 4)   E = (-1, -5)   F = (3, 0)

G = (-1, 3)   H = (2, -5)   I = (1, 3)

Page 59:   Area and Perimeter

1. P=52 A=80
2. P=28 A=27.3
3. P=30 A=56

4. P=40 A=84
5. P=30 A=30
6. P=28 A=40

7. P=51 A=125.14
8. P=20 A=16
9. P=38 A=72

10. P=21 A=21.22
11. P=20 A=16
12. P=42 A=80

13. P=28 A=28
14. P=39 A=66
15. P=32 A=33

16. P=58 A=154
17. P=58 A=142.5
18. P=45 A=82.5

19. P=46 A=132
20. P=60 A=135
21. P=48 A=110.85

22. P=38 A=78
23. P=58 A=136
24. P=53 A=120

25. P=48 A=120
26. P=19 A=11.46
27. P=39 A=66

28. P=39 A=70.78

Page 66:   Pythagorean Theorem

1. S=143.384
2. S=48.754
3. S=96.747
4. S=49.960
5. S=105.551

6. S=110.725
7. S=40.485
8. S=101.750
9. S=53.963
10. S=35.875

11. S=136.850 **12.** S=57.306 **13.** S=166.565 **14.** S=52.077 **15.** S=240.707

16. S=45.651 **17.** S=52.479 **18.** S=17.464 **19.** S=49.528 **20.** S=27.839

Page 71:   Volume and Surface Area

1. V=34 cm³ cm³ SA=50 cm² cm²

2. V=100 in³ in³ SA=130 in² in²

3. V=14 ft³ ft³ SA=28 ft² ft²

4. V=572.56 cm³ cm³ SA=382 cm² cm²

5. V=113.10 ft³ ft³ SA=132 ft² ft²

6. V=168 cm³ cm³ SA=188 cm² cm²

7. V=792 in³ in³ SA=518 in² in²

8. V=197.92 ft³ ft³ SA=188 ft² ft²

9. V=4 cm³ cm³ SA=13 cm² cm²

10. V=210 cm³ cm³ SA=214 cm² cm²

11. V=378 cm³ cm³ SA=318 cm² cm²

12. V=46 cm³ cm³ SA=78 cm² cm²

13. V=18 in³ in³ SA=42 in² in²

14. V=251.33 cm³ cm³ SA=226 cm² cm²

15. V=18 cm³ cm³ SA=42 cm² cm²

16. V=12 in³ in³ SA=32 in² in²

17. V=48 in³ in³ SA=80 in² in²

18. V=47 in³ in³ SA=83 in² in²

19. V=12 in³ in³ SA=32 in² in²

20. V=48 in³ in³ SA=80 in² in²

21. V=20 in³ in³ SA=50 in² in²

22. V=502.65 in³ in³ SA=352 in² in²

23. V=33 in³ in³ SA=64 in² in²

24. V=810 in³ in³ SA=522 in² in²

25. V=315 in³ in³ SA=286 in² in²

26. V=80 in³ in³ SA=112 in² in²

27. V=180 ft³ ft³ SA=192 ft² ft²

28. V=105 in³ in³ SA=142 in² in²

Page 78:   Mean, Median, Mode, and Range

1. Mean = 51.333, Median = 55, Mode = none, Range = 75

2. Mean = 58, Median = 72, Mode = 72, Range = 87

3. Mean = 36, Median = 27, Mode = 24, Range = 68

4. Mean = 44.667, Median = 52, Mode = none, Range = 94

5. Mean = 38.429, Median = 23, Mode = 15, Range = 83

6. Mean = 33.333, Median = 31.5, Mode = none, Range = 51

7. Mean = 46.429, Median = 57, Mode = none, Range = 88

8. Mean = 65.857, Median = 77, Mode = none, Range = 76

9. Mean = 35.833, Median = 29, Mode = 29, Range = 61

10. Mean = 50.714, Median = 56, Mode = none, Range = 55

11. Mean = 43.714, Median = 50, Mode = none, Range = 72

12. Mean = 67.857, Median = 79, Mode = 79, Range = 96

13. Mean = 56.333, Median = 54.5, Mode = none, Range = 79

14. Mean = 49, Median = 45, Mode = none, Range = 85

15. Mean = 55, Median = 58, Mode = 58, Range = 95

16. Mean = 63.667, Median = 78.5, Mode = 82, Range = 71

17. Mean = 49.167, Median = 42.5, Mode = 31, Range = 45

18. Mean = 54.667, Median = 56, Mode = none, Range = 49

19. Mean = 58.571, Median = 68, Mode = 78, Range = 67

www.ingramcontent.com/pod-product-compliance
Lightning Source LLC
Chambersburg PA
CBHW080835160726
47999CB00009B/2900